THE odd duck ALMANAC

AT HOME
ISSUE
FARMFLIX

ALMANAC

EDITED BY ADAM BOLES

ILLUSTRATIONS BY SHELBY CRISWELL
PHOTOGRAPHS BY RICHARD CASTEEL

BROUGHT TO YOU BY

odd duck

barley SWINE **sour duck**

CATTYWAMPUS PRESS, AUSTIN

The Odd Duck Almanac

Printed in USA
First edition

ISBN 978-1-7340625-3-3

Cattywampus Press
7421 Burnet Road, #164
Austin, TX 78210
contact@cattywampuspress.com

Editor: Adam Boles
Illustrator: Shelby Criswell
Photographer: Richard Casteel
Art Direction, Design & Typesetting: Lindsay Starr
Sponsoring Editor: Daedelus Hoffman

Printed, bound, and distributed by OneTouchPoint, Austin.

CONTENTS

LETTER FROM THE EDITOR

Maybe it's a little on the nose, but for my 2020 summer reading, I decided to tackle Stephen King's *The Stand*. It's a doorstop of a book about a ragtag group of people trying to navigate the dystopian hellscape brought about by a global pandemic—or, as we might call it, a prophecy of current events. The novel was published the same year I was born, 1979. I write to you from the afternoon of another scorcher at the end of August in Austin, I find myself only days away from my 41st birthday.

It's important that you know exactly when I wrote this letter because of something else Stephen King says in another of his books, *On Writing*, a terrific memoir and treatise on craft. In it, he describes writing as an act of literal time travel. He posits that, as I write to you today, I am actually projecting myself into the future, along with all my hopes, worries, and questions, many of which you, as my reader in the year 2021 or beyond, already have answers to. Will they find a solution to this virus? Who will win the upcoming election? Are we going to be okay? You know better than I.

Perhaps it's because of the funny qualities time has taken on this year—the way a week can feel like a month, or how the days fuzz together—that makes this project of writing, compiling, and editing the second volume of *The Odd Duck Almanac* feel like such a privilege. In these pages, I've attempted to chronicle a singular time in our collective experience, and do so in a decidedly unique format. Beyond being a cookbook and informational guide, this is a yearbook of sorts, too.

Conceived of as an annual publication, the *Almanac* is tasked with telling the story of the year gone by, the story of the food and community and ideas that passed through the kitchens and dining rooms of this ever-evolving restaurant family. When I accepted this assignment, I didn't think that the product of my labor would be anything like what you're holding in your hands.

Back in January, when the guys asked me to take this on, they were gearing up for another great year at their three restaurants. They had already picked a theme for this volume, and I set to work sketching out that book (which still lives in the vault, and will hopefully see the light of day in a future edition. Who knows? Maybe from your place on the timeline, it already has). We were well into the initial drafting stages when things went sideways. In rapid succession, South by Southwest was canceled, then the whole city—the whole world, really—went into lockdown.

I don't need to tell you that the ensuing months have been harrowing. Leaving aside the chaos of current geopolitics and widespread social unrest, the impact of the pandemic on restaurants is too much for any of us at this vantage point to get our arms around yet. But for Bryce, Dylan, Mark, and Jason—the partners behind the restaurants featured herein—all of this upheaval has actually played to some of their biggest strengths, both as artists and businesspeople.

Every day, Bryce and his cooks take the ingredients available during a particular season and allow themselves to be guided by what they have to work with. It's an honest way to cook, and, for an artist, constraints like this can actually open up worlds of invention. These guys work best when they're pushed into corners and forced to improvise their way out. I took a cue from their creative philosophy and decided: if this is a yearbook, then it's our job to tell the very specific story of this unorthodox year.

To do that, we decided to take the book largely out of the restaurants and into a place we've all been spending a lot more time recently: our homes. This is where we've cooked most, if not all our meals this year. It's where we taught ourselves to bake bread for the first time, or where we turned a spare bedroom into an *ad hoc* yoga studio. Home is where we've struggled to find yet another engaging activity for the kids, and where, if we're lucky, we've kindled the embers of our relationships. This has been a year of personal reinvention for a lot of us, and a year where sometimes a batch of chocolate chip cookies is all that stands between us and madness.

This has been a year of personal reinvention for a lot of us, and a year where sometimes a batch of chocolate chip cookies is all that stands between us and madness.

As a cookbook, this volume often asks you to choose your own adventure. A lot of the recipes talk to each other, so don't be surprised if you're flipping from front to back and everywhere in between when cooking a dish. Many of the recipes are blank slates, basic starting points inviting you to bring your own personal signatures to them.

First and foremost, this book is meant to be useful and accessible to you, to teach you a few tricks in the kitchen, and to give you strategies for how to live bountifully in this new reality. Beyond that, however, is a more subtextual aim: to point us toward a kinder, more sustainable path out of this mess.

While I would never suggest that living through this time is anything other than deeply challenging—a Stephen King novel come jarringly to life—I will say that it is an uncommon opportunity for a writer like me to be able to document a little ounce of history as it's happening. My perspective is unavoidably narrow. I'm not able to connect certain dots or make all the right choices because I don't have the benefit of the hindsight you've been gifted.

I have tried, however, to construct a decent time capsule, a bit of primary source material we can use to make sense of what we've lived through together. Whatever the as-yet-unknown outcomes are, we can be sure that all of us will be recalling 2020 for the rest of our lives. And I'm positive those recollections will sound something like, "Can you believe we made it through all that crazy bullshit?"

The story of 2020 isn't done being told, at least not from way back here. But the story we tell in this book tries to tap into the currents of our moment, currents of resilience and community, of conviction and adaptability. It speaks to a very human impulse many of us embraced this year—that, even when the world is at its bleakest, we can still somehow manage to create delicious, even beautiful things. It is beauty that nourishes us as much as food, and beauty that gives us the hope we need to take another step forward.

Be well,

Adam Boles
Editor

PREFACE

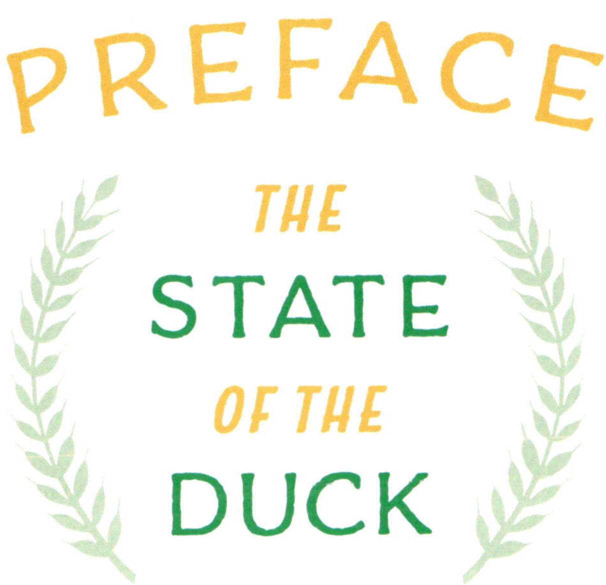

THE STATE OF THE DUCK

BY BRYCE GILMORE,
EXECUTIVE CHEF & PARTNER

I ended my essay to you in the last edition of the *Almanac* by talking about the big-picture philosophies of our restaurants. I said that our mission with our food is to tell the story "of a particular place at a specific time and the talented people making it happen." Despite the yo-yo swings of opening and closing our restaurants over and over this year, the heartbreak of furloughing our beloved staff, and the anxiety and uncertainty we've felt as the wider world explodes around us, we remain true to our mission. And 2020 has given us quite a story to tell.

Something you should know about me: I'm a very optimistic person. When you start your own business, you kind of have to be. Even if you've thought everything through and planned it all out, you're still taking a giant leap of faith. You're not only making an investment in yourself, but you're also investing in your community—your staff, your partners, and the people who support your ideas. All successful

Left to right, from top left: Kat holds a Paloma-to-go at Odd Duck. The Sour Duck Neighborhood Market offerings during qurantine closures. Bryce and Daniel behind the line at Odd Duck. Kevin prepares take-out orders at Barley Swine. Carlos, Gab, and Frida hold a cinnamon roll log before it's cut to make buns.

restaurant owners know you have to fight for your business. It's a much harder fight right now, but there's always a fight to some degree. So, I have a lot of hope, even if sometimes it feels like hope is pretty much all we have. I can't get down on myself or too upset because we're still here and I believe we're gonna be fine.

Holding on to that belief has definitely been difficult at times. Since the start of the pandemic and the first lockdown, we've had to rethink what we do on a daily basis—like, *every day*. We're constantly faced with questions you usually only have to answer once when you open a restaurant for the first time. How should we set up the dining room? Do we offer to-go service? What's the right path to maximize efficiency? We're also faced with a bunch of new questions, most importantly—how do we keep the loyal, dedicated people who come to work in these new conditions safe and healthy?

If I'm totally honest with you, that's been the hardest part in all this. A good number of our staff are really scared, and with good reason. We ask so much of them to come back to work so that we can continue to operate, knowing they're putting their lives and their households' lives at risk. That is the worst part of this whole situation: the feeling that I'm forcing people to make that decision. I hate being in that position.

We're going to keep fighting because that's what we know how to do.

I could go on about how I wish this crisis had been handled differently at the outset, how maybe Texas should've stayed closed for longer to try and knock this thing out, but that didn't happen, so here we are. All I can do is try to grow and learn and be grateful for what we do have. I remind myself that a lot of my colleagues and friends in this industry are in a lot worse shape than we are, and we have a lot to be thankful for.

In spite of all the challenges this year, we still managed to cook some really good food. At the beginning of this, we pivoted Barely Swine from a fine-dining restaurant to a commissary kitchen where we produced to-go feasts to feed the whole family. Check out the "Family Meal: A Backyard Barley-Q" chapter for our tribute to that effort.

Sour Duck became an actual market for awhile, selling goods and produce from our local purveyors, which you'll see featured throughout this book. And because we can never get enough pastry in our lives, we began delivering "Bake Boxes" from Sour Duck because it turns out cookies can make most things better, even if just for a short while. Flip over to the "Stress Baking" chapter to try your own hand at some great desserts.

Speaking of Sour Duck, shout out to my partner and brand new dad, Mark David Buley, whose wife had their first baby in July! Welcome to the club, Pop!

I also can't tell you how relieved I am that our farmers seem to be doing so well. Usually when a crisis hits, they're the ones who feel it first. Droughts or monsoons, fires or frosts, the farmers usually get hit hardest. Not this time. Even though the orders from restaurants dropped, every farmer I've talked to has said that the community at large has more than made up for any lost business. In fact, many of them are saying they're doing better now than they did last year. Some of our partners, like Jeff from I O Ranch, even gave us their surplus to use for staff meals which we cooked and boxed every day our restaurants had to be closed. You can't put a price on that level of kindness and generosity. There are silver linings everywhere. You just have to look for them.

The core of my optimism right now lies with our guests — with you. You've been absolutely tremendous throughout this mess. You've stuck with us, ordering to-go food, coming into the dining rooms and being respectful of all our new safety protocols. And the tips you're leaving for our staff are unbelievable and so appreciated. One of our regulars, Andrew Collins, even started a GoFundMe campaign to support our staff, helping to raise more than $7,000. It blows me away to see some of you donating hundreds of dollars without expecting anything in return. I know most of you aren't wealthy people, just normal folks trying to help us out because you like us. It feels really good to know that people are willing to sacrifice on their end to help keep us alive. The measurable difference you made for some really deserving people is just amazing. "Thank you" doesn't even begin begin to cover it, but it's a start—*thank you*!

It's hard to know what the future will bring for our restaurant family, but I do know that with the continued support of our wonderful Austin community and the hard work of our dedicated staff, we're going to see the other side of this. We're going to keep fighting because that's what we know how to do.

THE Pantry

A great home cook is only as good as their ingredients, so we want to take a minute to talk about staples. Great quality flours, oils, and spices can mean the difference between a good dish and a dish that takes flight. Our first volume of *The Odd Duck Almanac* has a great bunch of pantry staples throughout. For this edition, we want to help get your larder fully stocked. ➜

BARTON SPRINGS MILL

We've been working with miller James Brown and his team since they first kicked their imported Austrian stone mill into gear back in 2017.

Not only do they produce the highest quality locally-sourced wheat, rye, and corn products, but they also supply seeds directly to their handpicked farmers all over Texas to produce grains of rare excellence. James works with other farmer friends of ours—like Jim at Richardson Farms in Rockdale—to revive ancient and heritage varietals, grains that were commonly grown in Texas a hundred years ago but have since gone nearly extinct. Thanks to Barton Springs Mill, those grains have made a huge comeback.

Corn

Corn is the spiritual base of our region's cuisine going back millennia. BSM offers an amazing selection—like the revived 19th century varietal Bloody Butcher red corn, or the centuries old Oaxacan green corn—in whole kernel, cornmeal, and grits.

Flour

We love experimenting in our kitchens with all the different varieties of flour available from BSM. Let's look at a few standouts:

ROUGE DE BORDEAUX

A heritage bread flour known for its nutty aroma. BSM's '00' Rouge de Bordeaux makes a great all-purpose stand-in, especially for breads and cookies.

RUBY LEE

We love using this organic whole wheat flour as a flavoring flour in our Hill Country Loaf.

SONORA '00'

We use Sonora '00', another great high-protein flour, in our Chocolate Chip Cookies (pg 54) at Sour Duck Market.

ALL-PURPOSE PREMIUM BLEND

This '00' mix of Rouge de Bordeaux and Sonora is a beautifully well-balanced AP flour great for most applications.

Good Flow Honey

Father-son team Tom and Daniel Crofut have been raising bees just south of Austin for more than 40 years. The honey they produce is about as pure an expression of our local environment as you can get, due in large part to the Crofuts' philosophy of beekeeping: "We must operate under the dictates of our planet."

Texas Olive Ranch

Back when we started our little farm-to-trailer operation, we used to buy Texas Olive Ranch olive oil out of the trunk of Josh Henry's car. Thanks to Josh and his dad Jim, Texas is now an internationally recognized hub for olive oil production, and Texas Olive Ranch remains the best of the best.

Rice

Known for its singular flavor and its versatility, Carolina Gold is the granddaddy of American rice varietals. Driven into near extinction during the Great Depression, CGR has had a renaissance over the past few decades.

Spice Rack

Spice rubs and seasonings create the foundation of flavor for many of the dishes in this volume. For most of these, we toast the whole spices together in a dry skillet until fragrant, about 4 minutes. We let them cool before grinding them to a powder in a spice grinder. Then we sift out the chunky bits and combine the fine powder with the other spices. Store in jelly jars, and make sure to label them.

BRYCE'S SPICEY SPICE

(PATENT PENDING)

Bryce puts this on just about everything. It's a great rub for grilled meat, terrific in a flour dredge for fried chicken, delicious toasted onto bread, or just sprinkle on top of a dish for an extra added *pow*. No toasting or grinding necessary for this one.

3 tbsp sweet paprika
3 tbsp cayenne
3 tbsp Garlic Powder (pg 26)
2 tbsp Onion Powder (pg 26)
2 tbsp white pepper, ground
2 tsp ground mustard
1 tsp MSG
1 tsp cumin, ground

It has been etched in stone forever.

BOIL SPICE

2 tbsp mustard seeds
2 tbsp coriander seeds
1 tbsp allspice berries
1 tbsp dill seed
2 tsp celery seed
2 to 3 whole cloves
1 large dried bay leaf
4 tbsp cayenne
2 tbsp Onion Powder (pg 26)
1½ tsp Garlic Powder (pg 26)

ESPRESSO POWDER

Take the used coffee grounds from your last pot and spread them out on a parchment-lined baking pan. Heat your oven to 170ºF, and dehydrate the used grounds for 2 to 3 hours, or until the grounds are dry and feel crispy and brittle. Using a spice grinder, grind into a fine powder. Sift to remove any chunky parts. Store in a jelly jar.

Add a pinch to anything chocolate to catapult your dessert to the next level. Espresso powder is great in savory spice rubs, too.

LAMB SPICE

This is a perfect rub for any game meat.

3 tbsp coriander seed
2 tsp cumin seed
1 tsp black pepper corn
2 tsp whole allspice
2 to 3 whole cloves
2 tsp ground cinnamon

NACHO SPICE

2 tbsp cumin seed
2 tbsp coriander seed
1 large dried bay leaf
2 tsp sweet paprika

PECAN SPICE

3 to 4 cinnamon sticks
2 to 3 whole cloves
1 tbsp ground ginger
4 tbsp coriander seeds
2 tbsp whole black
peppercorn

NANAMI TOGARASHI

This citrusy, spicy Japanese-style spice can be used as an all-purpose seasoning blend. It works particularly well sprinkled over grilled vegetables, rice, or eggs.

2 tbsp black sesame seeds
2 tbsp white sesame seeds
2 tbsp white peppercorns
2 tbsp pink peppercorns
2 tbsp Szechuan peppercorns
2 tbsp fennel seed
2 tbsp red chile flakes
Zest of 1 orange,
dried

Spread orange zest out on a parchment-lined baking sheet, and dry in a 200ºF oven for 20 to 30 minutes, or until the zest is hard and crumbly. Alternatively, you can use a food dehydrator following the manufacturer's instructions.

In a dry skillet, toast the white and black sesame seeds together over medium heat, about 5 minutes. Set aside. Toast the white peppercorns, Szechuan peppercorns, and fennel seeds together until fragrant. Let cool.

In a spice grinder, add the chile flakes, pink peppercorns, dried orange zest, and toasted spices. Using a spice grinder, grind into a chunky powder, then add the toasted sesame seeds. No need to sift this one.

QUICK PICKLE BRINE

This basic brine will get you started pickling anything your little heart desires. Feel free to experiment flavoring your brine with spices like peppercorns, whole coriander, fennel seeds, chile flakes, and mustard seeds. You can also include fresh herbs like dill and thyme. White wine and rice wine vinegars are nice substitutes for white vinegar.

1 cup white vinegar
½ cup water
1 tbsp sugar
1 tsp kosher salt

Bring water to a simmer, then add the sugar and salt, stirring to dissolve. Remove from heat and add the vinegar. Pour hot brine over any veggies you want to pickle, and include any pickling spices or herbs with the veg.

PICKLED MUSTARD SEEDS

Use as a garnish on plates with grilled meat, fish, or vegetables. Great anywhere mustard is called for.

½ cup yellow mustard seeds
1 Quick Pickle Brine recipe

Put the mustard seeds in a small sauce pot and cover with water. Bring to a boil, then reduce heat and simmer for 5 minutes. Strain and repeat 2 to 3 times to mellow the flavor of the mustard seeds.

Bring Quick Pickle Brine to a boil and add the cooked mustard seeds. Reduce heat and simmer for 5 to 10 more minutes, until the seeds are plump and softened. Transfer to a canning jar. Cool and refrigerate overnight before enjoying.

MEAT BRINE

Great for poultry, game, or lean pork. An overnight soak will tenderize the meat and keep it from drying out when you cook.

1 gallon water
100g (½ cup) brown sugar, packed
230g (¾ cup) kosher salt

Combine all ingredients in a stock pot over medium-high heat, stirring until the salt and sugar are dissolved. Let cool before brining your meat.

CHILE PASTE

3 cups water
2 cups white vinegar
125g Guajillo chiles
100g Ancho chilles
25g Arbol chiles
50g Morita or Chipotle chiles

Destem all the chile peppers. Boil water and vinegar together, then remove from heat. Add the chiles to the hot liquid, cover and let steep for 15 minutes. Blend until smooth. Store in the fridge—it gets better with age.

FRIED GARLIC

Measure the ingredients by weight to achieve the correct proportions.

1 part garlic, diced
1 part sunflower oil
1 part olive oil

Add garlic and sunflower oil to a skillet and heat together over medium heat. Toast the garlic, stirring often, until it is golden brown. Be careful not to burn the garlic—it cooks quickly at the end. When ready, remove from heat and immediately add the olive oil to stop the garlic from cooking. Strain the garlic using a fine mesh sieve or chinois, reserving the oil. Spread the garlic on paper towels to cool completely. Store the fried garlic in the fridge in an airtight container for up to a month. Use the oil to cook with, make mayonnaise, or finish savory dishes.

GARLIC AND ONION POWDER

Making your own garlic and onion powders is super easy, and the product is so much more flavorful than that ancient dust you get at the supermarket.

Thinly slice the onions or garlic, and put them in a food dehydrator set at 130ºF. Drying times vary, but they could take as long as 24 hours to completely dry.

You can also use your oven set at the lowest temperature. Just lay out the onions or garlic in a single layer on a parchment-lined sheet, and stir every 30 minutes until done. This method takes less time, but requires more of your attention, and there is a danger of burning.

The alliums are done when they are dry enough to crumble between your fingers. Add them to a spice grinder and process into a fine powder. Sift out any chunky bits, and store in an airtight container.

HOUSE MAYO

This mayonnaise is the foundation upon which so much flavor is built. It's a blank slate, so dress it up with spices, infused oils, or anything else you can imagine.

- 2 egg yolks
- 1 tbsp lemon juice
- 1 tbsp Texas olive oil
- 2 tsp dijon mustard
- 1 tsp cold water
- ½ tsp kosher salt
- 1½ cups sunflower oil
- 1 garlic clove, grated on a microplane

In a stand mixer fitted with the whisk attachment running at medium speed, combine the egg yolks and the cold water, then add the lemon juice, dijon mustard, and grated garlic. Beat until frothy, then slowly add in the olive oil a few drops at a time. When the mayonnaise begins to thicken and emulsify, increase the speed, and slowly stream in the sunflower oil.

PUFFED RICE AND GRAINS

Sure, you can always go grab a box of puffed rice from the cereal aisle, but making your own is really easy. The first technique works for any kind of rice—short or long grain, and even wild rice—or you can use a similar technique to puff grains like sorghum, amaranth, and buckwheat. Puffed rice and grains are a great way to add a crunchy texture to both savory and sweet dishes.

Rice Technique

Cook rice as normal, allowing it to slightly overcook. Spread cooked rice on a baking sheet in an even layer and let it sit out over night at room temperature, uncovered. The rice is sufficiently dry right when the grain has become hard and slightly translucent.

Prepare an empty pot with a metal sieve and keep on a cold burner. In a medium saucepan, fill about halfway with a neutral, high-heat oil like sunflower or grapeseed oil. When the oil reaches 375ºF on an instant read thermometer, toss in a single grain of rice. If it puffs, your oil is ready.

Add rice to the oil and fry for 5 to 10 seconds until puffed. Carefully pour oil and rice through the metal sieve, straining the oil into the cold empty pot. Cool rice for 5 minutes.

Grain Technique

There are two viable approaches to puffing grains like buckwheat, amaranth, and sorghum. You can follow the puffed rice instructions from start to finish, replacing the rice with your grain of choice. The result will be a grain with a harder crunch, similar to a corn nut.

Alternatively, you can skip cooking the grain first and just add it to the oil raw. With this technique, your grain will be lighter and airier, something akin to popcorn.

To finish: Season or flavor however you want depending on the application. Toss with a Nanami Togarashi (pg 23) or Nacho Spice (pg 23) seasoning for savory applications. Powdered sugar, cinnamon, and cocoa powder are great flavorings for a crunchy dessert topping. Puffed rice and grains can be stored in an airtight container for up to a week.

HOUSE STOCK

We're always looking to cut down on food waste and make the most of our amazing local ingredients. One great way to do that is to make a house stock.

A house stock doesn't have any set ingredients. It is not strictly a chicken stock or a beef stock or a vegetable stock (unless you're a vegetarian cook). It's made of whatever leftover scraps, skins, end bits, stems, trimmings, and bones you've collected. Your stock is a very specific expression of yourself because it contains all the things that only you cook with and eat. No one else can make your house stock.

There are a few ways to think about making your house stock, and a few guidelines to follow. The first method will get your stock established, and the second will keep your stock going for months or years to come.

TECHNIQUE

For both methods below, we recommend you add a few bay leaves, some garlic cloves, a small handful of black peppercorns, and some dried or fresh herbs you may have lying around. Bring to a boil, then reduce to a simmer, and cook partially covered for 1 to 4 hours. Vegetable stock will take less time to cook than stock with a lot of bones in it. The longer the stock cooks, the more concentrated the flavor. If you choose to simmer your bones for a long period, we recommend adding any vegetables only in the last hour of cooking. Taste as you go, and wait until the stock is done but still hot to season it with salt. Once it's cooled, strain it through a fine mesh sieve or chinois, and refrigerate any you'll use in the next few days. Freeze the rest.

"ON THE FLY" HOUSE STOCK

Before you begin prepping for a meal you're going to cook, put a stock pot on the stove and fill it halfway with water. If you have any older stock in the fridge or freezer, pour that in there, too. Heat it gently, and when you're prepping your meal, put any scraps

into the pot as you go. When you're done prepping, make sure all the ingredients in the pot are submerged. Cook the stock while the rest of your meal cooks, then use it to make a sauce for your dish. The sauce will perfectly compliment whatever you've made because it will be flavored with the same ingredients.

LIVING HOUSE STOCK

In the same way your "on the fly" stock is an expression of the meal you made around it, your "living" stock is an expression of your overall culinary life. As you cook and eat, try to save any leftovers in a freezer bag. For instance, if you roast a chicken once a week, freeze any trimmings and bones. Freeze the ends of onions, corn cobs, Parmesan rinds, herb stems and other scraps you produce when making your meals. When you've filled up two gallon-sized freezer bags, it's time to make stock.

Thaw out any leftover stock from your last batch. Add the contents of your freezer bags to a large stock pot, then add the leftover stock. Fill the rest of the way with water and cook as described above.

This is a "living stock" because each new round of stock is an evolution of the last. The more generations you have, the deeper the flavors become, and the more particular the product is to you and your family.

**Note: when you see fortified stock in a recipe's list of ingredients, we are referring to this process of making stock with stock.*

SHOPPING LOCAL IN THE NOWTIMES

When the coronavirus pandemic first hit Austin back in March, 2020, a wave of panic buying struck local supermarkets and box stores. Long lines of socially distanced shoppers stretched around strip mall parking lots as the shelves inside were picked bare faster than stores could get in new stock.

At the same time, restaurants like ours were forced to close our doors to try and curb the spread of the virus. The immediate effects on restaurants were multiple and often devastating. As is true when any industry goes through a crisis, the ripples quickly spread far and wide. One of our biggest concerns became the fate of our farmers and other local purveyors.

"It was just going to be a normal March and April," said Carol Ann Sayle, longtime owner of East Austin institution Boggy Creek Farm. "Suddenly all the chefs and restaurants are shut down, and we're looking at each other saying, 'My God! What in the hell is going on? That's 40 percent of our business!'"

Finegan Ferrebouf and Jason Gold, owners of Steelbow Farm in Manor, Texas.

Carol Ann Sayle, owner of Boggy Creek Farm in East Austin.

Finegan Ferrebouf and her husband, Jason Gold, had just moved back to Austin in January to start Steelbow Farm. Their original business model was to supply restaurants exclusively. "Our first deliveries were to Barley Swine, Odd Duck, and Dai Due," said Finegan, whose newborn son Izzy was along for the ride. "It was the week before everything shut down. Our first delivery, and then it's like, 'And, we're done.'"

"For a couple days, I was really in shock. I just [felt like I'd] been kicked in the stomach," said Dorsey Barger of HausBar Farm. She and her wife, Susan Hausmann, have been selling their specialty produce to Austin restaurants for the past 11 years.

"I'd gone in and out of optimism and deep sadness, and this gut-punch feeling. So then I just said to myself, 'We are going to go all out on this. We are just shifting our entire focus immediately.'" Dorsey went to work setting up the infrastructure for her contactless pick-up, online-ordering "Farm to Neighbor" program.

For so many of our farmers, what started as a necessary pivot to retail sales during a moment of tumult has turned into one of the strongest years for farm sales in recent memory.

> **If there's a bright spot, perhaps it's that the trend away from supermarkets and toward locally sourced ingredients might be here to stay.**

"In April, we shifted to 90 percent retail from 90 percent wholesale," said Ty Wolosin of Windy Hill Farms. "[We] went to selling produce boxes, meat boxes, pantry goods, dairy—basically anything we could to help people out who could not get those goods, and keep some cash flow coming in. And it worked."

Almost across the board, our farmers reported an incredible uptick in demand from the public. Carol Ann and her daughter Tracy Geyer at Boggy Creek saw traffic at their farm stand increase by two and three times within a week of the shutdown. "It was the grocery stores that were falling apart," said Carol Ann, "and so people started coming. More and more folks had our food, and more and more people said, 'This is better than grocery stores!'"

Boggy Creek's farmstand also sells other locally sourced groceries. "We've increased our bought-in things," said Tracey. "We're trying to make it more of a complete shopping experience. Some people tell us this is the only place they buy their food from."

Owner, Ben McConnell, behind the Bouldin Food Forest booth at the Texas Farmers' Market at Mueller.

Our friends at Salt & Time and Dai Due—both locally sourced butchers and amazing restaurants in their own rights—made similar moves. They've successfully transformed into full-fledged grocers where they sell produce, meat, dairy, and dry goods sourced almost entirely from local purveyors.

"Right at the beginning, we got in with Salt & Time," said Finegan at Steelbow Farm, "and we've been selling a ton through [them]. They've been awesome partners."

Like many of our other farmers, Finegan and Jason also started a subscription box service they called "Veggie Boxes." Because their first planting was originally intended for Austin's best chefs, the produce they harvested in the spring included an assortment of fairly esoteric ingredients.

"Customers for the Veggie Boxes are excited to have something they wouldn't normally find on the grocery shelves," she said, pointing to items like Chinese stem lettuce (a.k.a. celtuce). "We tried to market to people who were willing to take on an adventure in the kitchen. That worked out really well."

If there's a bright spot to be found in the current *mêlée*, perhaps it's that the trend away from supermarkets and toward locally sourced ingredients might be here to stay.

"It's really amazing," said Tracy at Boggy Creek. "I don't know if it's because they're looking for stuff to do outdoors because it's safe, or if they're wanting a better source of food, or if they're scared of the grocery stores, or what it is, but we are still consistently—every day—having new people who come out here and buy food and walk around, and are just in awe of the place. I don't see it slowing down."

"We are going to make it," said Dorsey at HausBar. "Our neighbors have already shown us we can make it."

The pandemic exposed what many of us already suspected: the convenience that we've all come to rely on thanks to Big Ag and global supply chains might not be sustainable in this new world we're coming to know. Maybe it was never sustainable to begin with.

"We want everybody in the world to have the miracle of seeing something grow from the soil," said Carol Ann. "None of us are going anywhere because we are in the Earth, we are of the Earth, and we will never go away. And that's just the way it is."

HOW TO GET YOUR GROCERIES LOCALLY & SUSTAINABLY

It's easier than you think to source all your produce, meat, dairy, and other groceries from right here in Central Texas. In some cases, you can establish a direct relationship with specific farmers, but there are also plenty of markets and delivery services that allow for a more familiar shopping experience. Either way, you're supporting local agriculture and artisans which is good for farmers, good for your community, good for the planet, and good for you!

Farmers' Markets

Austin is home to some of the best farmers' markets in the country. A number of these outdoor markets happen all around Austin and Central Texas every week allowing you to shop directly from the producers. The Sustainable Food Center (SFC) hosts farmers' markets every Saturday in the heart of downtown and in Sunset Valley. The Texas Farmers' Market sets up shop in both Lakeline (Saturdays) and Mueller (Sundays). Farmers' markets are a great place to explore, get inspired, and meet the good people who grow and raise the best local food.

CSAs

Otherwise known as Consumer Supported Agriculture, CSAs are subscription boxes, usually offered weekly throughout harvest periods. Traditionally, these boxes are filled with veggies and herbs and other things grown on the farm. More recently, some of our partners, like Windy Hill Foods, are offering protein boxes with locally raised beef, pork, game, and other meats. Johnson's Backyard Garden has one of the longest running CSAs in the region, while Bouldin Food Forrest, VRDNT Farm, and Steelbow Farm are newer to the game.

Purveyor	CSA	Delivery	Stand
Barton Springs Mills		✌	
Boggy Creek Farm			☺
Bouldin Food Forest			
Farm to Table		✌	
Fruitful Hill Farm			☺
Good Flow Honey			
HausBar Farm	☼		
I O Ranch			
Johnson's Backyard Garden	☼		
Richardson Farms			
Steelbow Farm	☼		
Texas Olive Ranch		✌	
VRDNT Farm	☼		
Windy Hill	☼	✌	

See "Appendix B: Shopping Local Directory" on page 167 for more information about these fine local purveyors.

What's Available?	Where to Get the Goods?
Offering our favorite flour and grain products.	Pick some up at Sour Duck Market, Salt & Time, or find them at the Dripping Springs Farmers' Market. You can also order directly from them online.
Beyond the organic veg grown mere feet from the farm stand, they also feature products from many of our other local purveyors.	The Boggy Creek farm stand is an Austin institution. Come for the groceries, stay for Carol Anne's charm and wit.
Local, organic produce grown using sustainable permaculture systems.	Catch Ben and his team every week at the Texas Farmers' Market in Mueller.
Everything! Farm to Table partners with dozens of local purveyors.	Order online for their Austin-area home delivery service. They offer pre-packed Farm Boxes and a la carte groceries.
Veggies and eggs from this family operation.	This multi-generational family farm operates a farm stand Friday afternoons in Smithville. You can also catch them at Texas Farmers' Market Saturdays in Lakeline.
A variety of local honeys, including Wildflower, Mesquite, and Orange Blossom.	Available at most local organic grocers including the Wheatsville Co-Op.
High-end produce, herbs, and Dorsey's famous lettuces.	Check out their new Farm to Neighbor program, but you have to know the password (hint: it's hiding in plain sight elsewhere in this volume).
100% naturally raised, grass fed Dorper lamb	Find I O Ranch Lamb at Boggy Creek's magical farm stand. Also available at Wheatsville Co-Op stores.
A wide selection of seasonal produce.	You can find JBG Organics at pretty much every farmer's market in central Texas, and their CSA is among the most widely subscribed.
Humanely raised beef, pork, and poultry, as well as raw milk dairy.	Preorder for pick-up at a variety of local and regional farmer's markets.
Some of our favorite veggies	Visit their online store with preorder pick-up available, or sign up for a Veggie Box subscription when available.
The very best Texas grown and pressed olive oil	Order online at their site for delivery straight to your door.
Organically grown seasonal produce.	During harvest seasons, sign up for their curated CSA box.
GOAT!! And every other protein you can imagine.	If you ask nicely, farmer Ty Wolosin will happily add you to his weekly Meat Box mailing list, dropping off all over the region.

Products and availability subject to change.

Delivery

Grocery delivery services aren't exclusive to the big chain supermarkets. You can source all your groceries locally without ever stepping foot into a store. One of our main wholesale suppliers is a company called Farm to Table. Over the last year, they've opened their delivery service to the Austin community at large, selling just about anything you need to stock your fridge and pantry. They feature plenty of our partners, like Good Flow Honey, Texas Olive Ranch, and Mill-King Creamery, and they'll deliver directly to your home. Farmhouse Delivery is another great option, with offerings from producers like Hi-Fi Mycology, 44 Farms, Fruitful Hill Farm, and Bouldin Food Forest.

Farm Stands

If you want to actually see where your food comes from, take a visit to the farm. The good folks at Boggy Creek have been running their East Austin farm stand since 1992. Not only can you take home a selection of their delicious veggies, they also buy from other local producers, making it a one-stop shop.

Our friends at Fruitful Hill Farm also host a weekly farm stand on Friday afternoons, and it doesn't get much better than the beautiful produce they grow.

Local Grocers

When the pandemic hit, it wasn't only farmers scrambling to pivot their business models. Our friends at Salt & Time and Dai Due turned their restaurants/butcheries into full-fledged grocery stores. Not only can you find the best humanely raised or wild-caught meat at these two butcher shops, but now you can find regular grocery products like flour from Barton Springs Mill, and produce from a number of local farms.

If a more traditional supermarket experience is what you're after, the Wheatsville Co-Op has spent decades diligently sourcing their inventory from local producers. You can find products from our friends at I O Ranch, Windy Hill, and many others at their two stores in Central and South Austin.

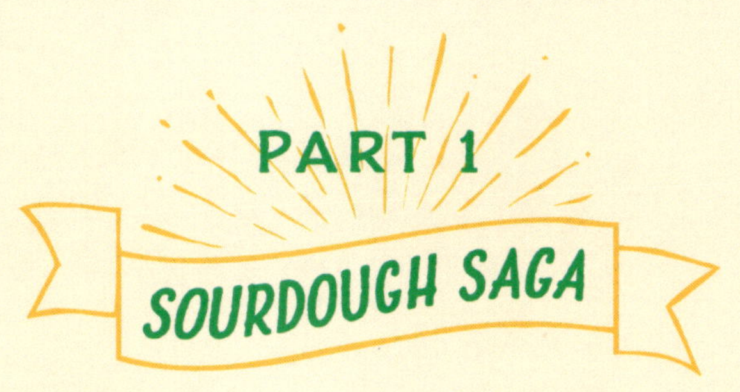

Getting Started

STARTING Your STARTER

THE JOURNEY TO HOMEMADE CRUSTY GOODNESS STARTS HERE

↓

What is sourdough starter?

Your sourdough starter tells a personal story about you and your environment. Just like everything else in the universe, sourdough starter is in constant flux, changing its attitude and demeanor in response to different times of year, its physical location, and what you've fed it to help it thrive. These qualities are expressed in how active it is, the ways it smells and tastes as it goes through its cycles, and the characteristics it imparts on the bread you bake with it.

More technically speaking,
your sourdough starter is an active fermentation, a colony of healthful lactobacilli bacteria and wild yeast. These bacteria and yeasts are found floating around in the air and exist naturally in flour, and they team up to form a symbiotic culture. After some back and forth with each other, the yeast produces carbon dioxide, which leavens your bread, while the lactobacilli produce lactic acid, which gives your bread its zippy flavor.

Simply put,
your sourdough starter is one of a kind. It is your unique fingerprint in a big wide world of bread making. No one else can produce your sourdough.

Mama, where does starter come from?

If you're lucky, you've got a friend or family member already on their sourdough journey, and you can just filch some of their starter and keep it going for yourself. If you're around East Austin, you can head over to Sour Duck Market and snag some dehydrated starter flakes to take home and reinvigorate. Either way, you're continuing a story started somewhere else, but you're taking over authorship by bringing the starter into your specific environment.

If you'd like to begin for yourself at the beginning, establishing your own starter from scratch is pretty easy. It just takes some attention and about a week's worth of time. Follow these instructions to create your own signature sourdough starter.

What do I need to start my starter?

Flour and water.

That's it. You will never need any more or less than these two basic ingredients to establish and maintain your starter. With these ingredients, you'll create an environment for life to grow and thrive — life that, if nurtured, can nourish you for years or even decades to come.

For simplicity's sake,

we've created the "Keep It 100" method of establishing and feeding your starter. We weigh out all the ingredients to 100g each, giving us a 1:1:1 ratio of flour, water, and seed starter. That way, if you get tired of so much discarded starter, you can scale down using that ratio.

To START your starter:

100g whole grain flour
100g water, room temperature

To FEED your starter:

100g unbleached all-purpose flour or bread flour
100g water, room temperature
100g seed starter

We're using a whole grain flour like whole wheat or whole rye to get started. Whole grain flours maintain their germ and bran layers which contain proteins and rich micronutrients for our yeast and bacteria to feast on. Once we've established our culture, we will switch to an unbleached all-purpose flour or protein-rich bread flour.

When we say room temperature, we're talking about an ambient temperature between around 70ºF and 78ºF. Cooler, and your stater will take longer to establish itself; warmer, and you endanger the life of the culture and risk damaging the gluten.

Consistency is key!

It's a good idea to set up a standard time of day to work with your starter. We suggest feeding yours in the morning while waiting for the coffee to brew. To make it super easy on yourself, weigh out your ingredients the night before, and leave them covered on your counter overnight. That way, the water will have plenty of time to come to room temperature before you need to work with it.

DAY ONE

Mix 100g of whole grain flour with 100g of water to make a gooey dough ball. Put it in a quart-sized mason jar with a loose fitting lid. Let it sit on your counter for 24 hours. If your kitchen is generally cooler than 70ºF, try putting the starter on top of your fridge.

DAY TWO

Weigh out 100g of yesterday's starter and discard the rest. Stir it into 100g of water, then mix in 100g of all-purpose flour. Put it back in its jar and let it rest for 24 hours. You may not see any bubbling or activity yet, but don't worry—life is happening!

DAY 3 to DAY 7-ish

By now, you're starting to see some bubbles forming, and the fruity, yeasty aromatics may begin to announce themselves (if not, just keep the faith and keep feeding!). Now it's time to double the feeding schedule. Repeat the steps in Day 2 every 12 hours for the next 5 to 12 days. For instance, if you do your first feeding at 7:00 a.m., then do your second feeding of the day at 7:00 p.m. It doesn't hurt to write the time of the last feeding on a piece of masking tape and stick it to the jar to help you keep track.

You'll know your starter is ready to rock n' roll when it doubles in size about 2 to 4 hours after a feeding. If you get to day 7 and the starter hasn't achieved this benchmark yet, just keep going. Establishing a rigorous and vibrant culture can take up to two weeks. Once ready, we'll call this your "seed starter."

Get to know your starter

We encourage you to get intimate with your starter, to learn its moods and subtle variations. Watch it for volume and bubbling. Smell and taste it often, and pay attention to where it is in the feeding cycle when you do. Is it bright and fruity with warm, yeasty aromas? Then you've got a vivacious, active starter feasting away on its most recent meal. Does it smell more like a distillery, or have sharp acidic notes? Then it's probably hungry and ready to feed.

There are infinite shades between these two poles, and your starter will behave in its own unique way. If you study and interact with your starter, ask questions of it, and maybe write down your observations in a log book, you'll develop a relationship with it. You'll get to understand its cycles, its needs, and when it's trying to tell you something it wants. This is why we often name our starters — they develop personalities, and likewise, we develop an emotional connection to them.

Carlita, the starter Mark Buley established all the way back in 2008, has been hard at work in our kitchens since we opened. Mark has daily rituals with the different versions of Carlita, and we think he actually has full conversations with her when he shows up alone to bake at 4 o'clock in the morning. This is totally normal and acceptable behavior, so just ignore your family if they look at you funny while you're chatting up a mason jar full of bubbly goo.

Now what?

Just like any other living thing in your care, you've got to feed your starter to keep it going. Use the "Keep It 100" method for a healthy, well-fed starter that will last as long as you want it to.

"Keep It 100" Feeding Method

- Weigh out 100g of mature starter, discard the rest.
- Mix that starter into 100g of room temperature water.
- Stir in 100g of flour until all of it is incorporated.
- Store in a quart-sized mason jar with a loose-fitting lid.
- If you bake more than once a week, leave it on your countertop and feed it every day.
- If you bake less often, stick it in the fridge. Pull it out and feed it once a week.

Waste not, want not

Don't just toss out your over-the-hill starter. It'll make a mess of your drain, and stink up your house like a brewery (though come to think of it, that might not be the worst thing). Try these instead:

Compost it! Just mix in enough water so it's the consistency of milk, then pour it into your compost heap.

Make something! Crackers and pretzels are terrific ways to turn your discard into snack-time gold. Or, try Mark's special English Muffins. Sourdough discard recipes are available on our website.

Dehydrate it! Simply feed it as described above, wait 3 to 4 hours, spread it all out on parchment, and let it get completely dry at room temperature. Break it into chips and store in an airtight container.

Skip ahead to page 59 to start making your own sourdough bread!

For the full digest version of the bread recipe, see page 163.

MY SPIRIT ANIMAL IS A DANISH PASTRY

A PRELUDE TO CARLOLINE'S KRINGLE

BY MARK DAVID BULEY

If there has been a silver lining to being a chef in 2020, it has been the gift of the opportunity for thoughtful reflection, a chance to thumb back the pages of my personal history and sift out the nuggets of meaning and moments where my culinary calling bound me. I've had the chance to rediscover family cooking traditions, retrace plates of hospitality, and resurrect the dishes I call home. →

The countries of our families' heritage guide the shuttle on the loom of our identity.

My training and experience as a chef have been deeply rooted in the savory side of the food equation. I have, however, noticed a pattern along the way that leaves me wondering whether I ended up on the wrong side of the kitchen, or missed a part of the discipline that calls me. Pastry chefs on vacation, creative differences with restaurant overlords, and cuts to restaurant staffing budgets have all spawned occasion for me to don "the substitute teacher of the pastry chef world." It's a title that fits me like a pair of old boots, light on glamor but worn in comfort. It's a professional identity with some room in it, room to float from school to school and dabble in the countless subjects of the culinary world.

A chef's professional identity consists primarily of two parts. The first is the influence of our education and professional masters, a hodgepodge of culinary lessons and tickets punched along a collection of hot lines that string together the fabric of a chef's professional pedigree.

The second, a deeper and perhaps more important part, is the influence of the person on the profession. The streams of influence converge at a crane's foot confluence of the biological and cultural elements that drive a chef's identity. The birthplace and geographical location of a chef's upbringing, and the web of threads tracing back in time to the countries of our families' heritage guide the shuttle on the loom of our identity.

For me, my search retraced a line from my matrilineal heritage through my Wisconsin birthplace to the roots of my cultural identity in the Danish baking tradition. My maternal great-grandmother, Caroline Damgaard Ammentorp was born in 1892 in north central Wisconsin as a first-generation American born of my Danish immigrant forebears. Her family chose that part of Wisconsin as the soft rolling hills and dense forests of jack pine and birch bore a familiar resemblance to their former Danish home.

My great-grandmother's life led her through a series of small midwestern towns and across multiple professions. Her professional exploration started in Luck, Wisconsin where she tried her hand at teaching before being run off by the unruly and pastoral temperaments of the Wisconsin farm boys she taught. She then set a course south to Des Moines, Iowa in hope that her position at Grand View College as the school's baker would provide a more natural fit. Caroline seemed to have found her true calling in the Danish college's bakeshop where she quickly earned a reputation of being a truly gifted baker. Her work with yeasted breads and the laminated dough of the Danish baking tradition earned her notable praise and the stuff of family legend.

My maternal grandmother, Ruth Wolfram, recalls, "She would bake rolls so light and tender that they would just about float off the pan." She goes on to express how truly special her mother's baking was, reminiscing that, "Anyone can stir up a cake or bake some cookies, but it takes real finesse to work with yeast."

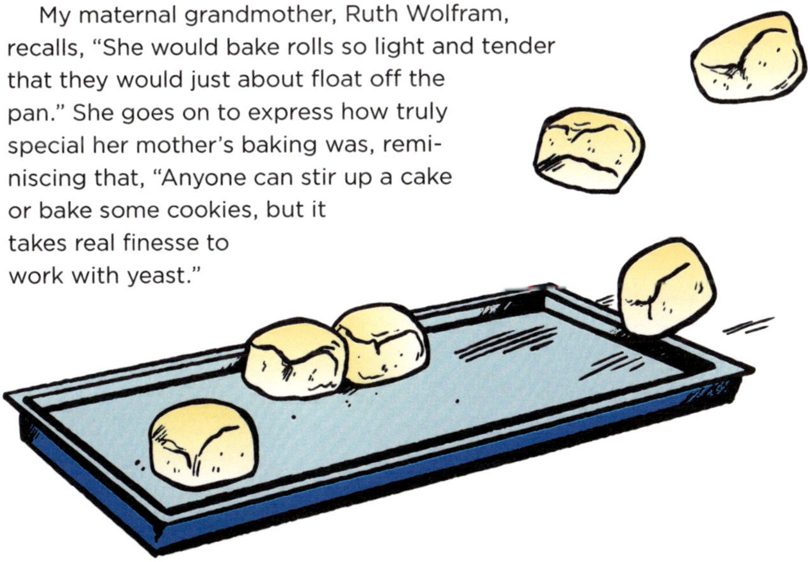

Nowhere was great-grandma Ammentorp's finesse more evident than in her renditions of the Danish classic Kringle, which just so happens to be the official state pastry of her Wisconsin home. Great-grandma Ammentorp's Kringle featured layers of yeasted dough laminated against thin sheets of sweet cream butter and punctuated by a stewed prune filling. The Kringle was the true family favorite.

A holiday or reflective conversation about great-grandma hardly passes without mention of her signature Kringles. Although I was never lucky enough to have tasted it myself, my family's stories and the collective memories of her written recipes have always piqued my curiosity. I often wondered if serendipity or some sort of family destiny would grant occasion for me to resurrect a now only fabled family baking tradition.

Little did I know that such an occasion would present itself in the most unlikely set of circumstances. The onset of the coronavirus pandemic, and the negative space that the campaign of social distancing created left me with some serious time for self-reflection. Wondering what the post-pandemic world would hold, I began to reflect on the road that brought me to restaurants and pushed me to baking in general. With my newfound surplus of free time, I began reading and researching my Danish roots and reimagining my role in our family's culinary story. A fateful phone call to my maternal grandmother set us reminiscing about great-grandma's baking. We settled in on the realization that her time baking at Grand View College had her baking straight through the Spanish Flu pandemic.

LEFT: Janet Buley, (*left*) and Caroline Damgaard Ammentorp (*right*).

RIGHT: Grand View College Old Main, Grand View, Des Moines, Iowa, c. 1910. Image courtesy of Wikimedia Commons.

The moment I got off the phone with my grandmother, an eerie sense of poignancy set in as I realized the depth of the parallels that bound our situations. The obligation to a sense of honoring and appreciating my family story took over and set me about searching for a greater understanding of how my ancestors had coped with such a pernicious situation.

A phone call to the Alumni office at Grand View University helped connect me to the school's archives and added some light and color to my understanding of the circumstances that my great-grandmother baked through. On October 10th, 1918, the Department of Health placed the entire city of Des Moines under quarantine. Dr. Woods Hutchenson advocated for the widespread use of "flu masks." On the tail the tail of the outbreak of over 3,000 cases at Camp Dodge just outside the city, the authorities heeded Dr. Hutchenson's advice, closing schools (Grand View included), and mandating the wearing of masks in public. The more I dug and studied, the more uncanny the parallels became.

Reflecting on the parallels felt almost like peering down the halls of history in a house of mirrors. With circumstances faced during the Spanish Flu so bleak, it left our ancestors, like us in 2020, with little choice but to turn to the simple pleasures to endure. They, too, found the therapeutics of the day inadequate: whiskey tinctures and turpentine rub was little more than placebo to numb the pain.

Like my great-grandmother, I turned to the familiar in coping. A sense of therapy sent me to the kitchen to bake. Putting my finger on the reason why may elude me, but I would venture to guess that my great-grandmother's reasons were the same. There is a structure and simplicity in baking. There is a comfort in the manifestation of caring that only fresh baking can bring. There is a hopefulness in the synergy of the mundane that can transform into the divine. There is a reassurance in predicting that a loaf will rise, and most importantly there is a connection within and across generations in a meal shared.

So, I find myself staring down the branches of my family tree and tracing the familiar curves of cursive that guide me through sheets of butter and layers of pastry to bake the family Kringle.

One recipe shared, one hundred years later and a pandemic apart.

To be continued . . .

The recipe for *Caroline's Kringle* will be shared in an upcoming Odd Duck Almanac Newsletter.

SUBSCRIBE TODAY AT ODDDUCKALMANAC.COM

Cooking WITH Your Ducklings

You made it through another week crushing at your job while simultaneously shepherding your kiddos through virtual schooling. It isn't just your broadband's bandwidth that's stretched thin. Thank goodness for the weekend when you can finally relax—except your kids are still stuck inside, and you remain on 24-hour entertainment duty! If you're struggling to find fun activities to keep the cabin fever at bay, try bringing the kids into the kitchen with you.

Cooking with your kids is more than a focused task to keep them busy. They learn about nutrition, and they gain a sense of agency in learning how to take care of themselves. They also pick up concepts in math and chemistry by encountering their real-world applications. Best of all, if you have picky eaters, cooking their own food demystifies what's on the plate, and might prompt them to try new things. At the end of it, they have a delicious trophy to show for their efforts that they can be proud of.

These fun recipes are family favorites, but don't limit yourself just to them. Bring your kids along for the experience of cooking anything in this book because you never know — your little kitchen helper might one day end up as our kitchen's sous chef.

GRANOLA

Granola is great to have on hand for breakfast or as a dessert topping, and fun to make with the kiddos. Feel free to play with combinations of different seeds and nuts—just keep the same proportions. Hemp and sunflower seeds work well, as do almonds. Shredded coconut can be added halfway through the baking process. You can also add dried fruit, chocolate chips, or other raw additions after the granola has cooled.

- 4 cups rolled oats
- 1 cup pecan pieces
- 1 cup raw pepitas
- ½ cup dark brown sugar, packed
- ¾ tsp fine sea salt
- 2 tbsp + 1½ tsp mesquite flour
- ½ tsp ground cinnamon
- 2 tbsp + 1 tsp honey
- 2 tbsp maple syrup
- ⅓ cup Texas olive oil

Mesquite flour is *made from the seed pod of the abundant mesquite trees found widely throughout Mexico and the southwestern United States.*

It is sweet and slightly nutty in flavor, and adds a nice depth of flavor to a dish. We use it in cookie dough and to flavor crème anglaise and meringues. You can source mesquite flour directly from Barton Springs Mill.

Heat your oven to 325ºF. Line a sheet pan with parchment or a silicon baking mat. In a mixing bowl, combine the oats, nuts, seeds, dark brown sugar, mesquite flour, cinnamon, and salt. Stir in the maple syrup, honey, and olive oil. Make sure everything is evenly coated. On the baking sheet, spread the granola in an even layer.

Bake for 25 to 30 minutes, stirring halfway through, until the granola is golden in color. Store in an airtight container as soon as it is completely cooled.

SOUR DUCK CHOCOLATE CHIP COOKIES

At Sour Duck Market, we use Sonora "00" flour from Barton Springs Mill for a nice structure and great chewiness. This recipe yields about 3 dozen cookies, but the dough balls freeze well, and it's pretty awesome to have them just waiting for you in your freezer for whenever you want homemade cookies. Just thaw out the dough balls before baking.

435g (3 cups) all-purpose flour
2 sticks of butter, room temperature
2 eggs, room temperature
200g (1 cup) organic sugar
200g (1 cup) dark brown sugar, packed
300g (2 cups) bittersweet chocolate, chopped; or bittersweet chocolate chips
6g (1 tsp) fine sea salt
5g (1 tsp) baking soda
Maldon or other flaky sea salt to garnish

Combine sugar, baking soda, and salt in the bowl of stand mixer, adding all the butter last. Using the paddle attachment, mix the butter into the sugar mixture on low until combined. Turn the speed up to medium and cream until light and fluffy, scraping the sides of the bowl and the paddle about halfway through, about 5 minutes total. Add vanilla, then add the eggs one at a time, completely mixing in one egg before you add the next. Scrape the sides of the bowl as needed to ensure uniformity. Don't over-beat.

On low speed, gradually add in the flour until the dough comes together and the flour is just incorporated. Remove the bowl from the stand mixer and fold in the chocolate by hand. Wrap dough in plastic and let rest at room temperature for 1 to 24 hours.

Heat your oven to 350ºF, and line a cookie sheet with parchment or a silicon baking mat. Scoop golf ball-sized dough balls and gently flatten them on the cookie sheet. Garnish with Maldon sea salt, and bake in batches of 8 to 10 cookies at a time. Bake for 12 to 15 minutes, rotating the cookie sheet halfway through. Cool for 5 minutes and enjoy.

SEASONAL FRUIT JAM

Making homemade jam is easy, but there's serious science happening under the surface. Maybe making this recipe can count as a chemistry credit for your kid's virtual home school assignments?

1 lb seasonal fruit, chopped into even pieces
½ lb (a heaping cup) sugar
Juice from 1 lemon
Pinch of salt

Combine fruit, sugar, lemon juice, and salt into a medium sauce pan and stir to combine. Let sit for 30 minutes to macerate the fruit. Bring to a simmer over medium heat. Reduce heat and simmer, stirring regularly to keep from scorching, about 30 minutes. Transfer to clean canning jars, leaving about an inch of headspace, and let cool before refrigerating. This jam keeps in the fridge for weeks, or months in the freezer. Alternatively, use the water bath method to can.

Chef Mark David Buley breaks it down:

Fruit itself is really just sugar bonded to aromatic compounds and expressions of soil mineral content. The lemon juice in the recipe will activate the fruit's natural pectin, and the maceration process will pull all the 'free water' out of the fruit, making the jam less susceptible to scorching.

MARK'S POPCORN

Popcorn is something of a lost art. Many of us were brought up on the steaming microwave bag of neon colored kernels. Real popcorn, however, couldn't be easier to make, and it's so much tastier than those other fakers. Here, we present something of an evolution of popcorn, from the basics to the classics.

¼ cup popping corn
2 tbsp sunflower oil
1 to 2 tbsp butter
Salt to taste
Hot sauce (optional)

Cover the bottom of a medium sauce pan with oil. Add 2 to 3 popcorn kernels, cover the pot, and set it over medium heat. When those kernels pop, the oil is hot and ready. Quickly add the rest of the popping corn and a knob of butter. If you like spice, add a few dashes of your favorite hot sauce. Cover the pot immediately and shake periodically through the popping process to keep the kernels moving. When the popping slows, remove from heat and let the last few kernels pop. Transfer to a bowl and toss with salt.

CARAMEL CORN

1 Popcorn recipe
1 cup brown sugar, packed
2 sticks of butter, cut into chunks
300g (⅔ cup) corn syrup
2 tsp kosher salt
1 tbsp vanilla

1. Heat your oven to 250ºF. Line a baking sheet with parchment or silicon baking mat.
2. In a small saucepan, melt the butter, then stir in the brown sugar, corn syrup, and salt. Over medium-high heat, bring the mixture to a boil without stirring. Remove from heat and cool until it stops bubbling. Add the vanilla.
3. Put the popcorn in a mixing bowl and drizzle the caramel over the popcorn, stirring to coat evenly. Spread out caramel pop-corn evenly on your lined baking sheet and bake until glazed and crispy, stirring every 15 minutes, about 45 minutes total.

CRACKER JACKS

1 Caramel Corn recipe
1 cup Spanish peanuts
½ tsp baking soda

Make the caramel corn recipe as described. At the end of step 2, stir in the baking soda with the vanilla. At step 3, mix the peanuts with the popcorn before drizzling in the caramel. Finish the recipe as described.

HILL COUNTRY LOAF

You may have heard that even the best sourdough bread is composed of just three basic ingredients—flour, water, and salt. That's true, but we assert that there are two other ingredients that must be measured just as carefully for bread to be its best: *time* and *temperature*. We'll talk about temperature in a bit, but now let's talk about time. →

You are on your bread's watch, not the other way around. The most important moments in the development of your bread dough happen when you're not looking. They occur quietly as the levain matures, the dough proofs, and the bread bakes. Learning when to intercede, for how long, and what you need to do in those short bursts of activity is the balance that even the most experienced bakers are eternally trying to achieve. You cannot force or rush the process. You must surrender to its clock.

Because time is such an important ingredient, we're presenting our sourdough recipe as a schedule. The bakers at Sour Duck Market show up at 4:00 a.m. to begin feeding and shaping. They bake throughout the day, and only complete their last feedings at around 10:00 p.m.

We allow for a more leisurely pace with the at-home recipe, extending the process out over two nights. This is a great schedule to keep if Day 2 falls on a Saturday or Sunday, or a day when you don't have to be away from the kitchen for too long through the morning.

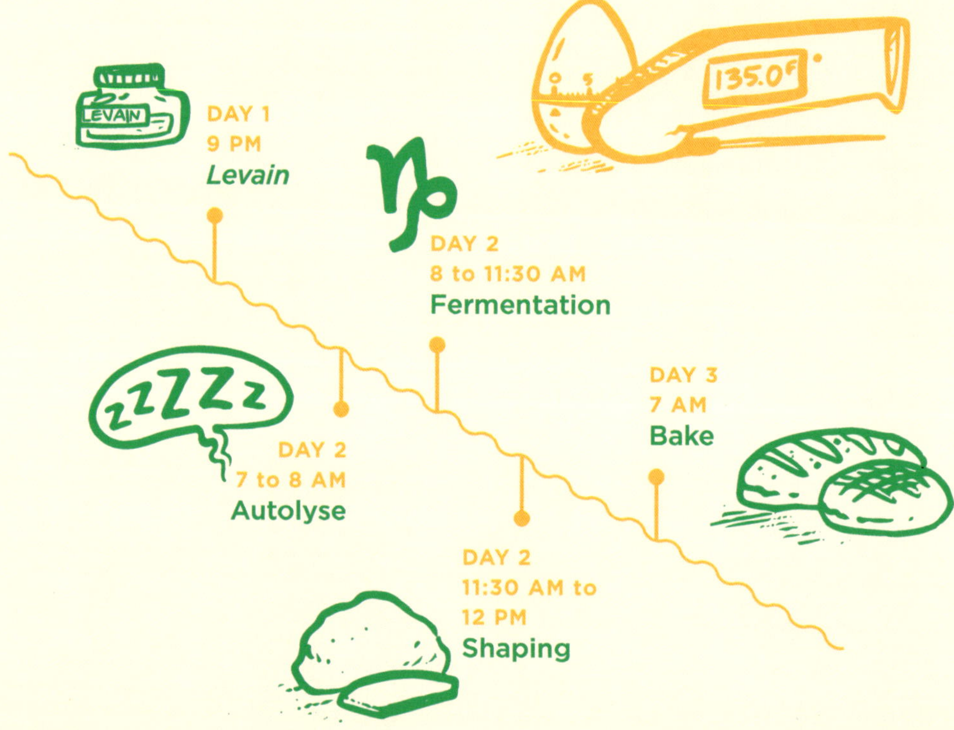

START

DAY 1, 9:00 p.m.

Now that our starter is alive and kicking, it's time to put it to use. The first thing we're going to do is—make more starter! Let's call the starter you feed regularly your *seed starter*. We'll use that to make the *levain*, the foundation starter for the bread you're going to make.

The timing for this levain is based on the idea that you bake for yourself about once a week, and you keep your starter in the refrigerator. Use your seed starter straight out of the fridge, and make sure to feed it as normal before putting it back.

If your seed starter lives on your countertop, make sure you feed it 3 to 4 hours before building the levain. In this case, your levain will be ready to use in more like 4 hours, not 10. The levain is ready once it has doubled in size.

10-hour *Levain*

We recommend Barton Springs Mill's Premium AP blend for the bread flour, and their Ruby Lee whole wheat as the whole grain flour.

- 50g bread flour
- 50g whole wheat flour, unsifted
- 100g water, room temperature
- 10g mature seed starter, cold

Mix the seed starter and the water, then incorporate the flour. Leave on your counter overnight in a mason jar with a loose-fitting lid up to 10 hours.

Levain is just the fancy French word for—you guessed it—sourdough starter. We use it here to distinguish between your seed starter and the starter we're using for the bread recipe.

To sift, or not to sift?

The reason whole wheat flour is more nutritious than processed white flour is that it retains its bran and germ layers, which contain much of the grain's protein and micronutrients.

When you build your levain, you want to feed your starter with all of those proteins and micronutrients, which is why we don't sift that whole wheat flour. With your dough, however, you want to sift the whole wheat flour to remove the bran layer so the flour can hydrate fully, resulting in a lighter, airier loaf of bread.

Get Ready for Tomorrow

Since you already have all your stuff out, might as well measure everything for tomorrow to make the morning go more quickly. Make sure you leave the water out over night, covered, so that it can come up to room temperature.

765g bread flour
160g whole wheat flour, sifted
635g water + 50g water, divided
20g fine sea salt

Skip to page 113 for the next step in the process, or see the whole recipe on page 163.

BY BRYCE GILMORE

As a chef, people always ask me what I cook at home. I think they assume I cook for my family the way I cook in my restaurants: small plates and tasting menus every night of the week! My wife, Molly, hears it, too—how lucky she is to be fed so well by her live-in chef-husband. In reality, we don't eat that much differently than you do. The whole point is to keep it simple, pretty healthy, and delicious. If you cook broccoli really well, for instance, and you season it right, it can be really good without being complicated. ➜

For me personally, one positive thing that's come out of the lockdowns and quarantines is being able to spend more time with my family. In more normal times, I work through meals most days of the week, so cooking for my family is a rare opportunity. Since all this started, I've had more dinners at home with Molly and Field, our five-year-old son, than I've ever had before, and I'm so grateful for it.

So, what do I make for them? We all eat the same thing, so I want it to be something we can all enjoy—straightforward, recognizable, and really tasty. For Field, I try to make sure there isn't too much stuff going on so he knows what he's eating. If he can't tell it's a carrot, he's less likely to try it. When I put three things on a plate for him, I'll make sure there's space between them. Kids want stuff separate!

Cooking like this is meant to be easy, something you can do in an hour with just a few ingredients. Easy clean up is the name of the game.

I also keep in mind that, unlike at the restaurant, I gotta do my own dishes, so I try to be smart about how I'm using my pots and pans. I have one big cast iron skillet, and I can pretty much cook a whole meal in that one pan.

Finally, I always think about what Mama used to make. Her chicken fried steak is a family tradition—we are Texans after all. Her cobbler was a staple in our house growing up, too. She's from Fredericksburg, so peaches are in our DNA. My dad always had that peach cobbler on his menus, and a version of it regularly pops up at my restaurants, too.

Cooking like this is meant to be easy, something you can do in an hour with just a few ingredients. Easy clean up is the name of the game. That way, you've made something the whole family can enjoy, and you'll still have time to actually hang out with each other.

WE LOVE . . .

made·in

Our mission at our restaurants is to source as much as we can from local Central Texas businesses. That includes the equipment we use in our kitchens. Lucky for us, Made In—among the country's preeminent manufacturers of professional knives, carbon steel and stainless clad cookware—is based right here in Austin. The same high-quality Made In kitchenware we cook with every night is also available to you directly from the company at their website, **madeincookware.com**.

HONEY KOMBUCHA GLAZED CARROTS

These are Field's favorite. The honey brings out the natural sweetness of the carrots, while the kombucha adds a little zip of acidity for balance.

6 to 8 medium carrots, large dice or oblique cut
3 tbsp butter
3 tbsp honey
2 tbsp fresh thyme, picked
½ cup kombucha
kosher salt, to taste

In a large skillet over medium heat, melt the butter and add the carrots, tossing to coat. Cook until carrots begin to soften and brown. Stir in the honey and cook until carrots begin to caramelize. Add kombucha, bring to a simmer, and reduce to a glaze. When the carrots are *al dente*, season with salt and thyme.

made

FIREPLACE CHARRED BROCCOLI

I never want to let a good fire go to waste, so I cook in my fireplace at home all the time. If you don't have a fireplace, a charcoal grill will work just fine. The key is cooking directly on the coals, and to keep the broccoli moving like a stir fry.

4 cups broccoli florets
some good Texas olive oil
half of a lemon, zest and juice
a handful of Italian parsley, chopped
1 tbsp Fried Garlic (pg 25)
2 tbsp fried garlic oil
salt to taste

Start a fire in your fireplace. When you have an ashy bed of coals, heat a perforated steel grilling pan directly on them. Toss the broccoli in olive oil and add half of it to the hot grill pan. Stir often, until the broccoli is just cooked and charred. Cook the broccoli in two batches, then toss with the lemon juice and zest, fried garlic oil, and parsley. Garnish with fried garlic, and season with salt to taste.

spatch·cock

/'spaCH,käk/

Origin : Irish

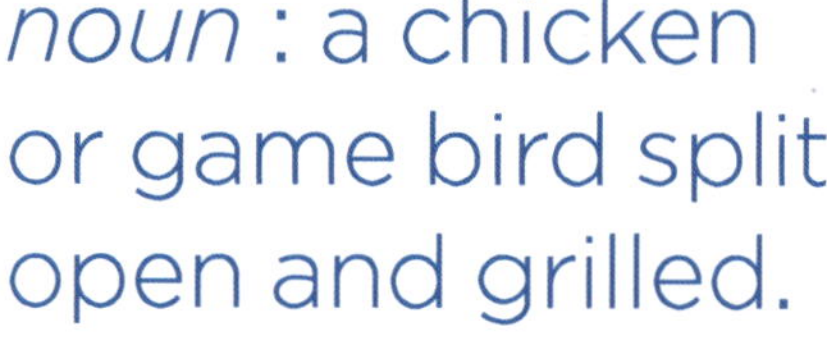

noun : a chicken or game bird split open and grilled.

GRILLED SPATCHCOCK CHICKEN

When roasting a whole chicken seems too complicated, try this method instead. The skin is crispy, the meat nice and juicy, and it takes a fraction of the time. If you're cooking on the fly, skip the brine and just season with salt and *Bryce's Spicey Spice* (pg 21).

Using poultry shears or a heavy knife or cleaver, remove the backbone from a whole chicken. Split the breastbone from the inside of the chicken so that the bird opens and lays flat. Meat Brine (pg 24) overnight. Remove from brine in the morning, pat dry, and chill uncovered in the fridge.

About an hour before you're ready to cook, season the bird all over with Bryce's Spicey Spice. Rest in the fridge uncovered for an hour.

Heat your grill. Over low heat, grill the chicken skin-side down until nicely browned. Flip and finish cooking skin-side up, uncovered over low heat. You'll know it's done when the skin begins to pull away from the bone at the bottom of the legs. Let the bird rest for 5 to 10 minutes before carving.

CHICKEN FRIED BONE-IN RIBEYE, MAMA'S STYLE

We wouldn't be Gilmores if we didn't mess with perfection. Sub out the tough old cube steak with a bone-in ribeye to bring this Texas tradition to the next level.

1 1½-inch thick bone-in ribeye steak
2 cups all-purpose flour
2 tbsp Bryce's Spicey Spice (pg 21)
1 egg
2 tbsp water or beer
4 cups milk
1 garlic clove, grated on a microplane
sunflower oil
salt and pepper

Season the steak generously with salt and pepper. Heat your oven to 225ºF and roast the steak in a cast iron skillet until the internal temperature hits 120ºF, about 25 minutes. Let rest on a rack for 30 minutes. Reserve the skillet with the rendered beef fat in it.

Mix the flour and Bryce's Spicey Spice together. Whisk the egg and the water or beer together. Add sunflower oil to the beef fat so it covers the bottom of the skillet. Heat over medium until 350ºF. Dredge the steak in the flour mixture, then the flour again. Reserve the flour dredge. Pan fry the steak on both sides until golden brown, about 5 to 6 minutes per side for a medium-rare steak. Let it rest on a rack while you make the gravy.

While the steak rests, pour all the fat out of the skillet, then measure ¼ cup of fat and return it to the skillet. Measure ½ cup of the flour dredge. Over medium heat, whisk the flour mixture into the fat. Cook the roux for 5 minutes, whisking constantly, making sure to scrape up any fond stuck to the bottom of the skillet. Add milk and grated garlic, bring to a simmer, and whisk until thick. Season the gravy with salt and pepper, ladle over the steak, and serve.

CAROLINA GOLD RICE

There are about 100 different ways to cook rice, but this method is great for adding a little extra flavor to any long grain rice. If you use Carolina Gold, however, you might not need to—on its own, Carolina Gold is the most flavorful rice you've ever tasted.

10 cups water
2 cups Carolina Gold Rice
2 sprigs rosemary, cut into thirds
¼ cup bacon fat or butter
salt and pepper to taste

Heat your oven to 300ºF. Melt the butter or bacon fat and set aside. In a stockpot with a lid, bring the water to a boil. Add the rice, cover, and return to the boil, then reduce the heat and simmer for 15 minutes, until just cooked. Strain off the water and spread the rice out on a parchment-lined baking sheet. Scatter the rosemary sprigs and drizzle the melted fat over top. Season with salt and pepper, then bake for 5 minutes. Remove the rosemary sprigs, stir, and serve.

MAMA'S CAST IRON "NEVER STIR" COBBLER

Sure, peach cobbler is the gold standard, especially for us Central Texans, but this crisp can be made with any seasonal fruit. Think apples in the fall and strawberries in the spring, or substitute other summer fruit like nectarines, plums, and berries in the summertime. Add some fresh Texas tarragon—also known as Mexican mint marigold—for a bright counterpoint to the sweetness of the peaches.

- 6 peaches, sliced
- 1 stick of butter, cubed
- 1 cup water
- 1½ cups all-purpose flour
- ¾ cup granulated sugar
- ¼ cup brown sugar, packed
- ½ tsp baking powder
- ¼ tsp baking soda
- ½ tsp cinnamon, divided in half
- pinch of salt
- 1 small handful of fresh Texas tarragon, picked and torn
- 1 tbsp Demerara sugar

Heat oven to 350ºF. In a large cast iron skillet, spread the peaches in an even layer and dust with ½ cup of sugar. Dot with butter, sprinkle with half the cinnamon, and set aside.

Mix the rest of the dry ingredients together. Sprinkle the dry mix over the peaches evenly, followed by most of the Texas tarragon.

Using your fingers, sprinkle the water over top of everything so it's evenly distributed. Top with Demerara sugar and the other half of the cinnamon. Bake for 35 to 40 minutes, turning the skillet once about halfway through.

Serve with a scoop of vanilla ice cream, and garnish with fresh Texas tarragon.

GROW YOUR OWN FOOD
By: TRISHA SUTTON
FROM SELF-WATERING GARDEN BOX TO URBAN FARM PLOTTING
TRISHA SUTTON FOUNDED URBAN AMERICAN FARMER TO CULTIVATE PASSIONATE PARTICIPANTS IN OUR LOCAL FOOD SYSTEMS.
CHECK OUT @URBANAMERICANFARMER ON INSTAGRAM TO ORDER HER NEW SEASONAL 'ZINE,
WHAT TO GROW AND COOK IN AUSTIN

GROWING FOOD IS A LIFE-LONG LEARNING EXPERIENCE. WHETHER YOU ARE A NEW GARDENER OR A FARMER, THERE IS SOMETHING TO LEARN EVERY DAY. WHEN WE GARDEN, WE NEGOTIATE WITH THE EARTH IN EXCHANGE FOR OUR MEAL. IT IS A DANCE WE DO WITH JOY AND ANTICIPATION OF THE HARVEST AHEAD.

YOU CAN GROW YOUR OWN FOOD!

BUT DO YOU WANT TO?
HERE ARE 3 GOOD REASONS TO TRY IT:

NUTRITION

VEGETABLES HAVE THE MOST NUTRIENTS WHEN THEY ARE FIRST HARVESTED.

HEALTH

WORKING WITH PLANTS REDUCES ANXIETY AND IMPROVES MOOD.

COMMUNITY

WHEN OTHERS SEE YOU GARDENING, THEY ARE LIKELY TO TRY IT, TOO.

BEGINNER

ORDER FORM ON BACK!

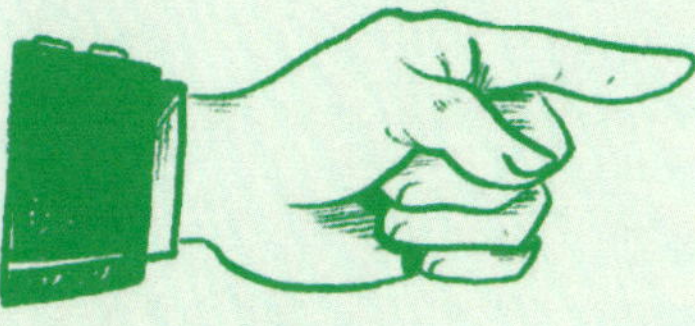

$75 PER BOX

LOOKING FOR A FUN ACTIVITY FOR YOUR FAMILY? WANT TO LEARN MORE ABOUT GARDENING? URBAN AMERICAN FARMER DESIGNED THIS SELF-WATERING GARDEN BOX TO MAKE GROWING AND HARVESTING YOUR OWN FOOD EASY AND ACCESSIBLE FOR EVERYONE. PERFECT FOR APARTMENT PATIOS OR YARDS WITH LIMITED SPACE. "SO EASY A KID COULD DO IT!"

- PLANT WITH TRANSPLANTS
- WATER ONCE PER WEEK
- FILL THROUGH THE PIPE UNTIL WATER COMES OUT OF THE DRAIN
- AT THE END OF THE SEASON, PULL OUT THE DEAD PLANTS AND START AGAIN!

ORDER SHEET

THE URBAN AMERICAN FARMER, AUSTIN, TX

MAIL TO:

5018 WESTFIELD DR
AUSTIN, TX 78731

DATE __________ 20______

OR URBANAMERICANFARMER@GMAIL.COM

** Fill out carefully. Write plainly. Thank you. **

NAME: ______________________________

PHONE NO.: ______________________________

STREET ADDRESS: ______________________________

CITY: ______________________________

→Delivery in city of Austin Only.

☐ DELIVERY ☐ PICK-UP (IN ALLENDALE)

I WOULD LIKE TO ORDER __________ (QUANTITY) SELF-WATERING GARDEN BOXES, FULLY PLANTED WITH SEASONAL HERBS & VEGETABLES FOR AUSTIN, TX.

I HAVE ENCLOSED A CHECK FOR $__________ OR SENT PAYMENT VIA VENMO @createurbanfarms

INTERMEDIATE
RAISED BED GARDEN
WHEN YOU'RE READY TO DEDICATE A SMALL PATCH OF LAND
N YOUR YARD, YOU CAN ESTABLISH A RAISED
ED GARDEN. IF YOU BUILD YOUR OWN, USE
EDAR BOARDS AND SUPPORTS INSTEAD OF
RESSURE TREATED LUMBER. CEDAR IS NATURALLY
OT-RESISTANT AND WON'T LEACH CHEMICALS INTO
UR FOOD'S SOIL. CHOOSE A LOCATION THAT GETS 8
OURS OF DIRECT SUN, PREFERABLY IN THE FIRST
RT OF THE DAY.
• BUILD A RAISED BED OR BUY PRE-FAB MODEL
• LINE THE BASE WITH CARDBOARD OR NEWSPAPER
• FILL WITH ORGANIC RAISED BED SOIL AND RAKE IN ONE BAG OF COMPOST
• PLANT WITH SEEDS AND TRANSPLANTS
• KEEP THE SOIL DAMP UNTIL THE SEEDS SPROUT
• WATER WHEN DRY, AN INCH BELOW THE SURFACE

ADVANCED
URBAN FARM
IF THOSE RAISED BEDS YOU BUILT DON'T PRODUCE ENOUGH TO SUIT YOUR NEEDS, IT MIGHT BE TIME TO REPURPOSE A BIGGER PATCH OF LAND FOR GROWING FOOD. TRY TO LOCATE YOUR PLOT IN A SUNNY SPOT THAT HAS READY ACCESS TO IRRIGATION. CHECK OUT THE TEXAS A&M AGRILIFE EXTENSION SITE FOR RESOURCES AROUND COMPANION PLANTING, WATERING & FERTILIZATION, ORGANIC PEST CONTROL, AND SO MUCH MORE.
USE A TILLER TO TILL UP A SECTION OF YOUR YARD. A PITCHFORK CAN HELP LOOSEN AND AERATE THE SOIL.

REMOVE GRASS & ROCKS, AND RAKE SOIL INTO ROWS.
ADD A THIN LAYER OF COMPOST TO EACH ROW.
COMPOST
PLANT WITH SEEDS OR TRANSPLANTS.
ADD DRIP LINE IRRIGATION OR OVERHEAD SPRINKLERS FOR CONSISTENT WATERING.

AUTUMN (OCT / NOV)

•ARTICHOKES •BOK CHOY
•BEETS •BROCCOLI •BRUSSEL SPROUTS
•CABBAGE •CARROTS •CAULIFLOWER
•SWISS CHARD •COLLARD •FAVA BEANS
•GARLIC •KALE •KOHLRABI •LEEKS
•LETTUCE •MUSTARD •ONION •PEAS •RADISH
•SHALLOT •SPINACH •TURNIP

WINTER (DEC–FEB)

•ARTICHOKE •BOK CHOY •BEETS
•BROCCOLI •CABBAGE •CARROTS •CAULIFLOWER
•SWISS CHARD •COLLARDS •FAVA BEANS •KALE
•KOHLRABI •LEEKS •LETTUCE •MUSTARD
•ONION •PEAS •POTATO •RADISH
•SPINACH •TURNIP

SPRING (MAR–MAY)

•CANTALOUPE •SNAP BEANS •BEETS
•SWISS CHARD •CUCUMBER •EGGPLANTS
•OKRA •PEPPERS •PUMPKINS
•SUMMER SQUASH •TOMATOES •WATERMELON
•COW PEAS •SWEET POTATOES

WET/COOL HERBS

•CHERVIL •CHIVES •CILANTRO •DILL
•FENNEL •TARRAGON •LAVENDER •PARSLEY
•SAGE •THYME •BORAGE •ROCKET/ARUGU

CALENDAR

HOT

SUMMER JUN-SEP

- OKRA
- COW PEAS
- IRISH POTATOES
- SWEET POTATOES
- PUMPKIN
- TOMATOES (LATE SUMMER)
- PEPPERS (LATE SUMMER)
- CUCUMBER (LATE SUMMER)

HOT HERBS

- CHIVES
- OREGANO
- BASIL
- LEMON BALM
- MINT
- LEMONGRASS
- ROSEMARY

*REMEMBER!

WATER DEEPLY AND LESS OFTEN

FOR THE SELF-WATERING GARDEN BOX OR 1-2 SMALL RAISED BEDS, BUY SOIL IN BAGS AT A NURSERY. FOR LARGER PROJECTS, BUY IN BULK FOR PICK-UP OR DELIVERY FROM WHITTLESEY LANDSCAPING. MIX SOME COMPOST INTO YOUR SOIL BEFORE EACH SESSION.

U.A.F's favorite Seed Companies

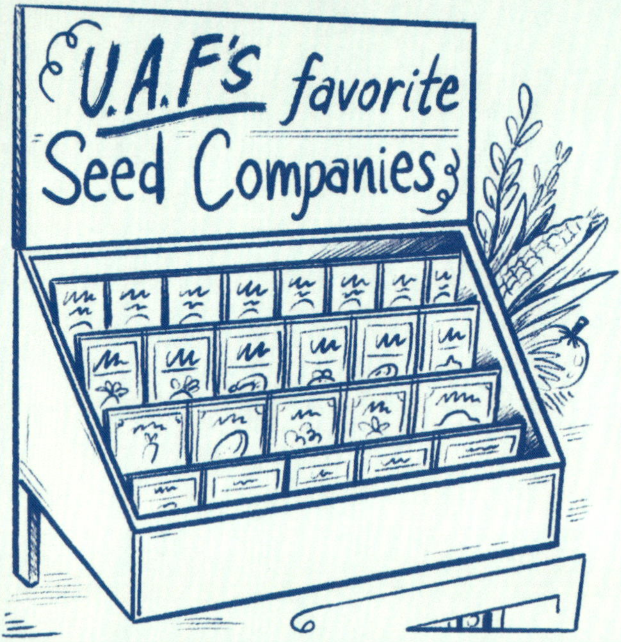

- FRUITION SEEDS
- SOUTHERN EXPOSURE SEED EXCHANGE
- NATIVE SEED SEARCH
- ROW 7 SEEDS
- BAKER'S CREEK
- SEED SAVER'S EXCHANGE
- RAVENSONG SEEDS & HERBS

WHERE TO BUY TRANSPLANTS AND SEEDS

- SHOAL CREEK NURSERY
- THE NATURAL GARDENER
- TILLERY STREET PLANT CO.
- WHEATSVILLE CO-OP

TAKING A WALK FOR SOCIAL JUSTICE

Zac Sagay has been working in the front of house with us at Odd Duck for three years now. Beyond being passionate about great food, he's our go-to guy for positive reinforcement, always armed with uplifting words or a welcome pat on the back. If you're bummed, Zac can usually find a way to make you feel pretty good about you. But he doesn't just talk the talk. In June, 2020, for his 34th birthday, Zac quite literally walked the walk—for 34 miles.

Despite knee surgery in February, Zac knew he wanted to use the day to give back to the community, but he wasn't sure exactly how to accomplish that. A fitness trainer and yoga instructor, he settled on a 34-mile fundraising walk—his doctors said running was out of the question—but who would it benefit? That's when he saw the post about fellow Austinite, Anthony Evans.

"I saw his story after the protests [in downtown Austin] against systemic racism and police brutality," said Zac. "He was injured while peacefully protesting. He was shot [in the face] with a rubber bullet." Mr. Evans's injuries were so severe he required a metal plate implanted in his skull, and to endure months with his jaw wired shut. Zac reached out to Mr. Evans over Instagram, and the two became fast friends.

"I told him, 'I know that money doesn't erase the trauma that you went through, but I want to support you however I can.' He's such an amazing person who's so full of love and compassion," Zac went on to say of Mr. Evans, "but he still has the energy to fight for justice. He didn't carry resentment or hate, and I was just really inspired by his response to a really tough situation. I don't know if I would've responded the same way if someone shot me in the face with a rubber bullet, to be honest with you."

For Zac, compassion and forgiveness have been hard won. When he was 22 and living in San Francisco, he was the victim of violent police brutality.

"It was the worst beating of my life, and it was at the hands of police," he said. "No one was held accountable.

"I was being taught a lesson," he continued, "and when someone treats you like that, it's really hard not to feel like that. I think I internalized that experience, and I didn't have the tools to process such a trauma when I was 22 years old. And that's just my story. I can't imagine how many other stories are untold or not documented and unseen, and I just don't want people to go through that."

This walk suddenly became more than just a fundraiser. For Zac, this was now personal.

The walk took place June 28th around Lady Bird Lake. The route looped them around the lake more than three times to hit 34 miles. Zac needed more than 8 hours to finish despite walking at "restaurant speed."

"[Odd Duck sommelier Kat Long] came by to show some support, and she was like, 'Damn, you're walking fast!' And I was like, 'This is crunch time! We're in the restaurant! It's 7 p.m. on a Friday! We gotta have that pace!'"

The fundraiser for Mr. Evans was a resounding success. They were able to add more than $6,000 to Mr. Evans's GoFundMe campaign to help him through his recovery. "Which is pretty awesome," said Zac.

"Beyond that, people showed up throughout the day of the event, and they got to meet [Anthony]. It was the community support and the love that he got to feel, which I just think is so much more powerful than any dollar amount, you know? After

I'm a lot more hopeful now because there are a lot of young people that are really fired up and are taking action, and that's a beautiful thing.

going through a trauma like that, to just feel loved and supported is so important."

Mr. Evans completed a good portion of the walk side by side with Zac. "I want to say he walked like 26 miles with his jaw wired shut, which is just crazy!"

Despite a few blisters and a purple toe, Zac and Anthony have developed a bond since their walk together. "It's just one of those fateful circumstances, coming across his story and his experience, that we connected, that it was personal for me, too."

For his part, Zac has recently completed his community yoga instructor training, and is planning to begin teaching yoga in prisons once pandemic restrictions have lifted. "My goal is to work on bringing mindfulness into prisons and jails, to help men forgive themselves and rediscover their inner light."

Even with all the uncertainty facing everyone these days, Zac stays true to form and maintains a positive outlook. "I'm a lot more hopeful now because there are a lot of young people who are really fired up and are taking action, and that's a beautiful thing."

As for how Zac celebrated the rest of his birthday after his 8 hour walk — "I had a double P. Terry's and fries right when I finished," he confessed. "And that was only the beginning! No shame!"

ZAC'S ANY TIME, ANYWHERE 7-MINUTE WORKOUT

BY ZAC SAGAY

We've all been spending so much time indoors and away from our normal lives, so for a lot of us I think it's been easy to get away from our fitness routines. Let's say your quarantine hasn't been as productive as you'd like, and you haven't been exercising much. Just the thought of an hour-long workout can keep you from jumping back into it. I always tell my clients that the key to getting and staying on track is simplicity and doing stuff you like. The most important thing is to start with something so easy that you can't fail.

One thing I've incorporated into my life is a seven minute workout every single day. I do this quick workout first thing in the morning before I eat anything. It's so good for kickstarting your metabolism to do a little exercise in a fasted state. That way, your body will reach for its fat reserves to burn for energy. And if this is the only exercise you get for your day, you'll have it out of the way first thing. Something is definitely a lot better than nothing!

The best thing you can do is learn to be intuitive with your body and feel it out. If pushups make your shoulder hurt today, then do some squats instead. Just listen to your body and start your day strong!

For this 7-minute workout, I choose 7 exercises at random. I do them for 30 seconds each, and I do that twice. It's all bodyweight resistance, so no equipment needed. When choosing exercises, I always try to pepper in a couple that raise the heart rate, like high knees or jumping jacks. You could even dance for 30 seconds. Put some music on! Mix it up! Make it weird!

This workout is just an example to get you started. Try to do different exercises and routines each day. Once you've mastered the 7-minute workout, add more exercises as you go, working up to 14 minutes. You'll be amazed at how much you can accomplish in such a short amount of time, and you'll feel great about yourself for having done it.

1. JUMPING JACKS

Standing up straight with your legs together and your arms at your sides, engage your core and put a slight bend in your knees.

Jump up, landing your feet a little wider than shoulder-width while touching your fingers overhead. Then jump back to your starting position. That is one repetition.

Keep your core tight, your knees soft, and stay on the balls of your feet.

2. AIR SQUATS

Stand with your feet between hip and shoulder-width apart, toes pointing forward. Put your arms out or overhead.

Keeping your chest up and your core engaged, breathe in as you squat down, sitting back with the weight in your heels, bringing your butt slightly lower than your knees. At the bottom of your squat, make sure your knees are behind your toes, and that your knees are not splaying out to the sides.

Push back up from your heels and your butt, keeping your core tight and breathing out as you rise up.

3. HIGH KNEES

Begin standing with a slight bend in your knees and your core engaged.

Start to run in place, using your core to bring your knees above your bellybutton. Aim to bring your knees to just under chest level. Stay on the balls of your feet, keep your chest up and your knees soft.

4. LEG RAISES

Lying on your mat, make sure your lower back is flat against the floor. Your arms should be at your sides with your palms facing down.

With your legs tight together, use your core to bring your legs up to 90 degrees. Bring them down with control, and don't let your heels touch the ground before starting your next rep. Try to get your heels as close to the floor as you can without arching your lower back.

5. LUNGES

From a standing position with your core engaged, take a big step forward with one leg so your heel hits the floor first before planting your foot.

Lower your body so your front thigh is parallel with the floor, and your front knee is behind or in line with your front toe. Aim to create a 90-degree angle with both legs, and don't let your back knee come all the way to the ground.

With your chest up and your core tight, push through your front heel to come back up to a standing position. Repeat with the other leg, alternating sides.

6. PUSHUPS

Starting in a plank position with your hands directly under your shoulders and your core engaged, make sure your shoulders, hips, and feet are in line.

Hug your elbows into your sides as you lower down and push back up. Try to keep your spine and neck in a straight line, and keep your hips from drooping.

Breathe in as you go down, and breathe out as you push up.

7. WALL SIT

With your back flat against the wall and your feet hip-width out in front of you, slide down the wall until your legs create a 90-degree angle.

Engage your core, tighten your butt, and squeeze your legs from your groin so your knees point forward and aren't splaying out to the sides. Hold this position for 30 seconds.

***Always consult your doctor before beginning any exercise routine. One size does not fit all, and the most important thing is for you to get healthy, not hurt!**

FAMILY MEAL

A BACKYARD BARLEY-Q

For so many of us, part of the appeal to working in restaurants are the relationships we form with our coworkers. We thrive in fast-paced, high-stress environments where the word "teamwork" is a laughable understatement. The connections we develop with each other don't lend themselves to easy classification. For lack of a better word, we are a unique kind of family with all the joys, conflicts, intimacies, and heartaches that go along with such a complicated and wonderful kinship.

Every night before service, the entire staff sits down together for Family Meal. Everyone from line cooks, dishwashers, and front of house staff to chefs and managers gather around a communal table to eat a meal together. It's the only time during a shift when we get to take a load off and relax, to commiserate and gossip, to nourish each other and ourselves. Frankly, it's one of the things we missed most when the pandemic forced us to close down this past spring.

Even when we weren't allowed to operate like we used to, family was at the forefront of our minds. We lost sleep thinking about the crew we had to temporarily furlough—if they weren't at work to make money and have a healthy meal, how would they get by? Our first order of business in the new reality was the same as everyone else's: we had to take care of our fam.

Through April, we enlisted skeleton crews to come in every day and cook Family Meal. We boxed it to-go and made it available for all of our furloughed staff to pick up. Some of our amazing farmers kicked in fresh meat and produce to help us feed our staff. Even if we couldn't enjoy a Family Meal together, at least we could make sure everyone had something delicious and sustaining every day.

When restrictions began to lift, we decided the best thing we could do for our Austin community would be to extend the sentiment of Family Meal to our guests. Instead of firing up our chef's tasting menu right away at Barley Swine, we decided instead to do weekly Family Meal feasts to-go. We went from serving delicately plated haute morsels to boxing whole smoked hogs and brownie sundaes for takeout. As summer set in, we coined the term "Barley-Q" to describe the smokey meats and grilled veggies we were turning out in Texas-sized portions.

What's so gratifying about working in hospitality is that we get to bring friends and family together around a table to help forge the bonds that make life worthwhile. Giving people that shared experience is at the heart of our mission, but these days we all have to be careful about how we do that.

If it's been too long since you've connected with your nearest and dearest, we want to offer this menu for your own summertime Backyard Barley-Q Family Meal. Hosting a meal outside is great way to safely bring people together, and feeding friends and family well will renew any waning connections stretched thin during quarantine.

This menu is designed to feed 8 to 12, and is meant not only to be served outside, but to be cooked in your backyard, as well. These recipes are presented individually, but check out the Menu Plan (pg 167) for instructions on how to prepare the whole menu without going crazy at the undertaking.

SOURDOUGH FOCACCIA BREAD

A great way to use your new sourdough starter, this savory, bubbly flatbread dough should be made a day ahead, but baked right before you're ready to serve.

350g (1 ½ cups) ripe sourdough starter
350g (1 ½ cups) lukewarm water (~100ºF)
750g (5 cups) all-purpose or bread flour
75g (⅓ cup) Texas olive oil, plus more for greasing and topping
20g (1 heaping tbsp) salt
40g (2 tbsp) honey
9g (1 tbsp) instant dry yeast

For the topping:
a few healthy pinches of flaky sea salt
a small handful of fresh rosemary, lightly chopped

Feed your starter a heavy meal about 4 hours before you're ready to make the dough—150g each of flour, room-temperature water, and unfed starter. It's ripe when it has doubled in size.

Mix the flour, salt, and yeast together, and set aside. In the bowl of a stand mixer, combine the ripe starter with the water. Using the dough hook attachment on the lowest speed, add the honey and olive oil, followed by the dry mix. Mix for 5 to 7 minutes until the dough is smooth and stretchy.

Autolyse: Transfer the dough to a large mixing bowl coated lightly with olive oil. Cover with a dishtowel and let rest for 1 hour on the counter.

Mix: After an hour, sprinkle salt evenly over the dough, then mix by gently folding the dough over itself 3 to 4 times. Cover with a dishtowel and let rise for 1 more hour, performing a ***Stretch & Fold*** (pg 116) after 30 minutes.

Bulk ferment: Grease a 13″ by 18″ sheet cake pan with olive oil. You can also use two 9″ by 13″ pans. Turn the dough out into the pan and gently stretch the dough into the corners. Cover and let rest for 15 minutes. The dough will contract as it relaxes. After the rest period, gently stretch the dough to the edges again. Repeat this process as necessary until the dough fills the pan edge-to-edge after a 15 minute rest. Cover the pan with plastic wrap and put it in the fridge overnight, 14 to 16 hours.

About 90 minutes before you're ready to serve the bread, heat your oven to 425ºF for at least 30 minutes. Remove the pan from the fridge. Use your fingertips to gently dimple the surface of the dough. Drizzle about an ounce of olive oil over top, then sprinkle with flaky salt and rosemary. Bake for 20 to 25 minutes until the bread is golden in color. Remove from the oven and let cool in the pan for 15 minutes. Turn the bread out of the pan and cut into squares. Serve warm.

SMOKED PORK LOIN

Brining the pork loin a day ahead will ensure juicy, flavorful meat that won't dry out when you smoke it. Be sure to reserve any trimmed fat to use when cooking your potatoes and dirty rice. Finally, consider smoking the pork loin early in the day before your barbecue, and then searing it on your grill *á la minute*.

4 to 5 lb pork loin roast
3 to 4 good handfuls of fresh herbs
  parsley, cilantro, basil
sunflower oil
salt and pepper

The day before your barbecue: Trim any excess fat from the roast, leaving a ¼-inch fat cap on the top. With a very sharp knife, score the fat cap in a crosshatch pattern about ⅛-inch deep. Prepare the Meat Brine (pg 24) recipe, and brine the roast overnight in the fridge.

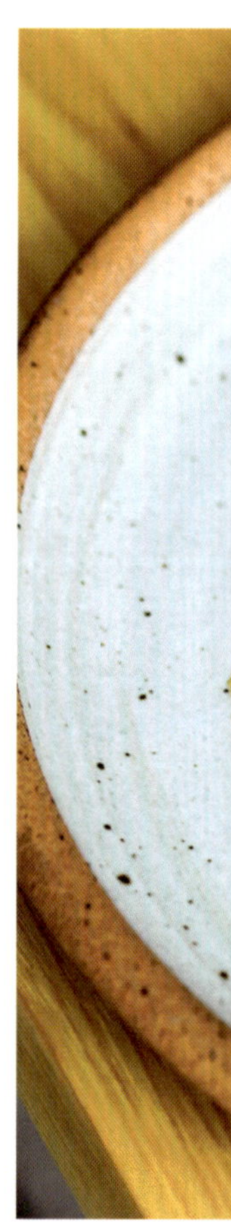

At least 3 to 4 hours before your barbecue: Preheat your smoker to 250ºF. Remove the pork loin from the brine and pat dry. Season all over with salt and pepper.

Add all the herbs to a food processor and turn it on. Drizzle in the sunflower oil until it forms a paste. Rub the roast all over with the herb paste.

Smoke the pork loin at 250ºF for about 2 hours, until an instant read thermometer reads 130ºF. Rest the roast for at least 20 minutes and then sear on a hot grill to caramelize, about 3 to 4 minutes per side. Slice and serve.

DIRTY RICE STUFFED QUAIL

We couldn't present a Texas-focused cookbook without featuring a recipe for one of our state's finest delicacies. We source our quail from Diamond H Ranch out of Bandera, Texas, and you can, too!

8 semi-boneless Texas quail
1½ cups Carolina Gold Rice
4½ cups water or stock, divided in half
1 lb ground beef
¾ lb bacon, ground or finely minced
1¼ lb chicken livers, ground or finely minced
8 oz pork fat (lard)
2 medium onions, small dice
1 bell pepper, small dice
4 garlic cloves, minced
1 to 2 jalapeño peppers, seeded and small dice
2 tbsp Boil Spice (pg 22)
1½ tsp sweet paprika
½ tsp Onion Powder (pg 26)
¼ tsp Garlic Powder (pg 26)
½ tsp MSG

The day before your barbecue: Prepare the Meat Brine (pg 24) recipe, and brine the quail for 4 hours.

Cook the Carolina Gold rice with half the water or stock. Bring to a boil, cover, and reduce to a simmer for 13 minutes. Remove from heat and leave covered to steam for an additional 5 minutes. Let cool then chill.

Grind together the beef, bacon, and chicken livers, and keep cold.

In a Dutch oven, heat the pork fat over medium heat. Once rendered, add the onions and sauté until glassy. Stir in the garlic and toast for another few minutes. Add the bell peppers and jalapeños and sauté for another minute, then stir in all the dry spices.

Turn up the heat and add the ground meat mixture. Stir until the meat has begun to cook and change color. Add in cooked rice and mix well. Add the other half of the stock, turn down the heat to low, cover and cook for 10 minutes. Remove from the heat and keep covered to steam for an additional 5 minutes. Cool before stuffing the quail.

Remove the quail from the brine and pat dry. Stuff each quail with about 2 oz of the dirty rice mixture. Tuck the wings behind the quail and tie the legs together to keep the stuffing in place. Chill uncovered in the refrigerator overnight.

At least 1 to 2 hours before your barbecue: Preheat your smoker to 250°F. Smoke the quail for 45 minutes to an hour, or until an instant read thermometer inserted in the stuffing-filled cavity reads 120ºF. Let rest for at least 10 minutes then sear on a hot grill on all sides to crisp and brown the skin.

GRILLED ZUCCHINI SALAD WITH GOAT CHEESE DRESSING

This grilled summer salad is packed with flavor thanks to the bright goat cheese dressing, fresh herbs, and crunchy toasted seeds.

3 medium zucchini
half an onion, sliced thin into half moons
a handful of fresh basil and mint, torn
zest of 1 lemon
enough olive oil to coat cooked zucchini
a few healthy dashes of red wine vinegar
salt, to taste
2 tbsp pumpkin seeds
2 tbsp sunflower seeds
1 tbsp sesame seeds

For the goat cheese dressing:
4 to 5 green onions
3 to 4 green garlic bulbs and stalks
⅔ cup chèvre
⅔ cup feta cheese
½ cup Texas olive oil
½ cup apple cider vinegar
1 tsp ground black pepper

To make the dressing: Grill green onions and green garlic until lightly charred and tender. Cool and finely chop. In a food processor, add chopped alliums, chèvre, feta, olive oil, apple cider vinegar, and black pepper. Blend until combined and uniform in texture. Can be made ahead.

In a dry skillet, toast the pumpkin, sunflower, and sesame seeds over high heat until brown and popping. Remove from the skillet and set aside.

Grill zucchini whole until charred and tender. Cool and cut into bitesized pieces, then toss with a few good pinches of kosher salt. Add sliced onion, basil and mint, lemon zest, olive oil, and red wine vinegar. Toss to coat.

Top the zucchini salad with the toasted seeds, and serve with a dollop of goat cheese dressing.

GRILLED SHISHITO POTATO SALAD

At the restaurant, we take the stems and seeds from grilled shishitos and infuse them into sunflower oil. If you're planning ahead, you can make the mayonnaise called for in this recipe with the shishito-infused oil to add another layer of flavor.

2½ lbs small Yukon Gold potatoes, halved
16 oz pork fat (lard)
12 sprigs of fresh rosemary
10 to 12 shishito peppers
1 cup House Mayo (pg 26)
3 tbsp Pickled Mustard Seeds (pg 24)
a small handful of fresh dill, picked
a good handful of baby arugula leaves

Confit the potatoes: Heat your oven to 225ºF. In a Dutch oven, render the pork fat over medium heat and let cool for 5 to 10 minutes. Add half the rosemary sprigs to the bottom of the Dutch oven, followed by the potatoes, then top with the remaining rosemary. You're looking for the fat to just cover the potatoes. Bake uncovered for 2 hours, then let the potatoes cool to room temperature in the fat. Discard the rosemary, but reserve the infused cooking oil to use again. Can be done a day ahead. Store the potatoes in the fat.

Grill shishitos on a hot grill until evenly charred. Destem and remove the seeds, then finely chop the charred shishitos. Stir chopped peppers into the mayonnaise.

Grill the confit potatoes until nicely browned, then toss them hot with the shishito mayo. Garnish with dill, pickled mustard seed, and arugula, and toss to loosely combine.

BUTTERMILK PIE WITH PICKLED PEACHES

It ain't summer in Texas without peaches. For this perfect summer dessert, we pickle the peaches to provide a tart counterpoint to the creamy buttermilk pie filling. If peaches aren't available, try substituting other summer stone fruit, like apricots, plums, or nectarines. This recipe makes two pies.

For the pie crusts:

300g (about 2½ sticks) butter, cold and cubed
350g (2½ cups) all-purpose flour
¾ tsp fine sea salt
½ tsp baking powder
6 to 7 oz ice water

For the pie filling:

6 eggs
660g (3¼ cups) sugar
52g (⅓ cup) all-purpose flour
485g (2 cups) low-fat buttermilk
2 sticks butter, melted
2 tbsp lemon juice
2 tsp vanilla
1 tsp sea salt

For the peaches:

4 to 5 ripe peaches, sliced
600g (3 cups) sugar
100g (½ cup) water
100g (½ cup) dry white wine
400g (1⅔ cup) apple cider vinegar
4 green cardamom pods
the peel of one orange

Pickle the peaches: Add water, wine, vinegar, sugar, cardamom, and orange peel to a sauce pot. Heat until the sugar is dissolved, then pour the hot liquid over the sliced peaches. Let cool and refrigerate. Can be made ahead.

Make the pie crusts: Measure cold water into a bowl, add 2 to 3 ice cubes, and put the bowl in the freezer while you do the next step.

Combine all the dry ingredients together, and divide the dry mix into ¾ and ¼ portions. Using a pastry cutter or two forks, cut the cold butter into ¾ of the dry mix until the dough is uniformly crumbly—the consistency of small peas. Add the rest of the dry mix and loosely combine.

Remove the ice water from the freezer. One tablespoon at a time, sprinkle the water over the dough mixture. Toss the mixture together lightly before adding the next tablespoon. Repeat for a total of 12 tablespoons of ice water.

Using a silicon spatula, scoop the dough from the bottom and fold over the top, pressing the dough together. Rotate your mixing bowl a quarter turn and repeat until the dough forms a ball. Turn and press as little as possible so as not to overwork the dough. If the dough is still too crumbly, sprinkle in more ice water a teaspoon at a time until it forms a smooth dough ball. Use a bench knife to divide the dough in half and wrap each dough ball in plastic wrap. Refrigerate for at least an hour.

Once chilled, roll the dough out on parchment, then use the parchment to flip your pie crust into a greased tart pan. Gently press the dough into the pan, and remove excess dough from the lip of the tart pan. Use a fork to prick the dough all over, including the sides. Repeat with second dough ball, then freeze both until firm.

Heat your oven to 375ºF. Remove the tart pans from the freezer, and cover them with parchment. Fill the tart pans with dry beans or pie weights. Bake for 10 minutes, rotate, and bake for 8 more minutes. Let cool completely with the parchment and weights in place. Once cool, remove the weights and continue baking the crusts uncovered for another 7 minutes.

Make the filling: Heat your oven to 400ºF. In a mixing bowl, combine the flour and salt. Whisk in the buttermilk and vanilla until smooth.

Using a stand mixer with the whisk attachment, beat the eggs with the sugar at medium speed. When the mixture has doubled in volume, reduce the speed and slowly stream in the melted butter. Once incorporated, slowly add the buttermilk mixture, followed by the lemon juice. Scrape down the sides of the bowl and make sure everything is well mixed.

Divide the filling evenly between the two pie crusts. Bake for 10 minutes at 400ºF, then reduce heat to 375ºF, rotate the pies and bake for another 15 minutes. Let cool completely before cutting. Serve topped with pickled peaches.

FROM THE ODD DUCK BEER BROS. JUSTIN, JEFF, & DAVE . . .

We recommend icing down a few sixers of Hops & Grain's The One They Call Zoe Pale Lager for a great barbecue beer. It's lightly hopped to cut through some of the fat on the pork, but light and crisp enough to enjoy on a hot Texas day.

OTHER LOCAL BREWS TO THROW IN THE COOLER

St. Elmo Brewing's Chico Pale Ale

The ABGB's Hell Yes Helles

Live Oak Brewing Company's Classic Pilz

AUSTIN MULE PITCHER

We love Austin's own Frankly Organic vodkas, but if you can't find them, feel free to use your favorite brand. The apple vodka is a nice touch, but not required to make a delicious cocktail.

Pro tip: If you have a juicer, juice some fresh ginger and turmeric roots and add a splash to each glass before pouring in the cocktail.

8 oz Frankly Organic apple vodka
6 oz Frankly Organic straight vodka
2 oz fresh lime juice
4 oz fresh lemon juice
1 oz Odd Simple (pg 140)
3 oz simple syrup
16 oz ginger beer
lime wheels from 2 to 3 limes

In a blender, add vodka, citrus juices, Odd Simple, and plain simple syrup. Blend for a few seconds until emulsified. Can be made ahead and stored in the fridge.

Add ice to a 32 oz pitcher and pour in the cocktail. Float lime wheels on top and reserve some for garnish.

To serve, add ice to a pint-sized mason jar (or copper mule mugs if you're being authentic about it). Fill about three-quarters of the way with the cocktail then top with about 2 oz of ginger beer. Garnish with a lime wheel.

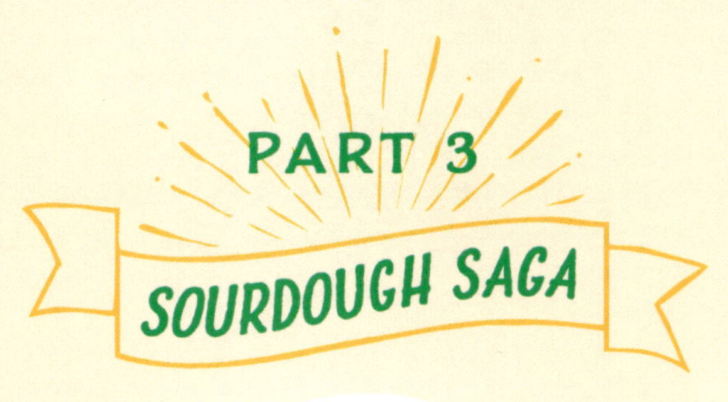

DAY 2, 7:00 – 8:00 a.m.

Autolyse

It's been 10 hours since you built your levain, and now it's time to put it to work. At this stage, you'll mix all your ingredients except the salt a little water, and then just let them be for half-an-hour. This resting period is called the *autolyse*, a pause in the dough-making process that allows the flour to fully hydrate.

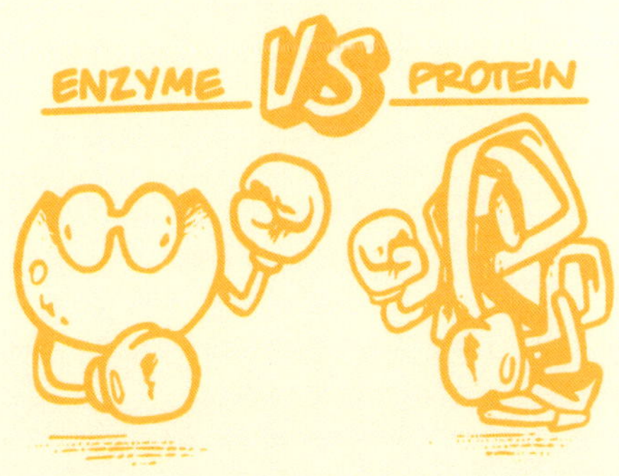

***The brief timeout provided by** an autolyse also allows the enzymes in flour to do some important work. They break down proteins in the flour to make the dough stretchier, and they turn the flour's starch into sugar for the yeast to consume. The result is dough that's easier to shape, and bread that has a more open and airy crumb.*

It's important to bring the levain, water, and flour together with wet hands. Keep a bowl of water next to your workspace so you can rewet your hands as needed.

In a mixing bowl, mix with wet hands 170g of levain with 635g of water (reserving 50g of water for later).

Fully incorporate all the flour until you have a shaggy, sticky dough ball.

Cover your mixing bowl with a dish towel and let it sit on your counter for 30 minutes.

Temperature

The other important ingredient in your sourdough is temperature. When the autolyse is complete, use an instant read thermometer to take the temperature of your dough. You're shooting for between 75º to 78ºF. If the dough is over or under that target range after an autolyse, you can use the 50g of reserved water to push it a degree or two in either direction. Make the water warmer or cooler than your target temp by 4 or 5 degrees, depending on which way you're trying to push the temperature.

Mix

After the autolyse, you'll find that the surface of your dough has taken on a markedly smoother appearance. To mix in the rest of your ingredients, just sprinkle the 20g of salt over the surface of the dough and pour in the last 50g of water. Massage the salt and water into the dough with wet hands, folding the dough over itself a few times until fully incorporated.

Now, take the temperature of the dough again. If the dough is still under 75ºF, keep kneading it for another few minutes. The warmth of your hands and the friction caused by the kneading will raise the temperature of the dough. If the dough is over 78ºF, put it in the fridge briefly to bring it down. Once you're in your target range, you can move on to the bulk fermentation phase.

8:00 – 11:30 a.m.

Bulk Fermentation

Bulk fermentation sounds labor intensive and intimidating, but really, there isn't much to it. After you've mixed in the salt and water, and your dough is about 75ºF, it's time to do nothing but wait. You'll need to stick around for a little dough stretching here and there, but otherwise it's the yeast and lactobacilli that are doing all the work.

Set a timer for 45 minutes, then perform a little dance we call the ***Stretch & Fold***. You'll do this three times over the course of bulk fermentation, every 45 minutes — at . . .

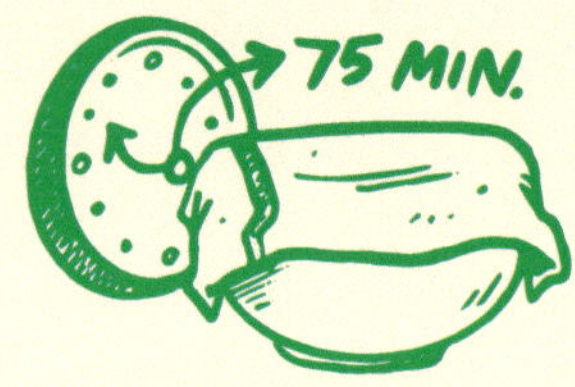

After your third ***Stretch & Fold*** shimmy, it's time to let the dough rest for about 75 minutes. This will allow the dough to increase in volume by as much as twice its original size.

How to Stretch & Fold

Stretching and folding your dough establishes its structure and elasticity. Throughout the shaping process, you're creating long, continuous strands of gluten. Allowing your dough to rest relaxes the gluten making it easier to shape.

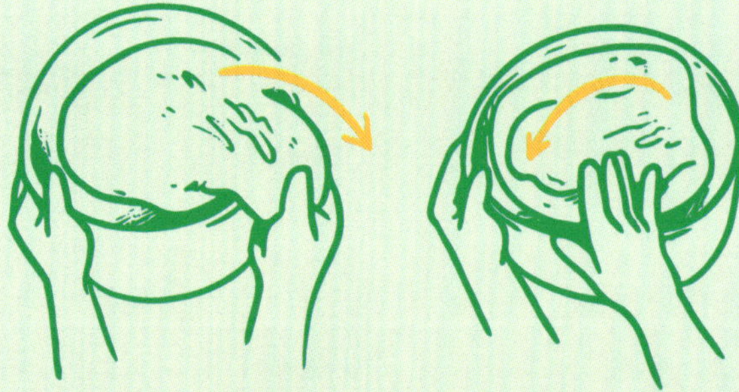

With wet hands, reach halfway under the dough ball, grab and ***STRETCH*** the dough back over the top and ***FOLD*** to the opposite side of the bowl, pushing the corners together firmly with your fingertips.

Rotate the bowl a quarter turn and repeat until you've made it all the way around the bowl once (four strectch-and-folds total).

11:30 a.m. – 12:00 p.m.

Shaping

It's important to move quickly and confidently when shaping your dough. In our previous steps, you were using wet hands to handle your dough. Now, you'll be working with floured hands.

If there's any step you'll find challenging, it's this one. You can watch endless YouTube videos by master bread makers deftly shaping their dough, but when you make your first attempts, you may feel ham-handed and clumsy in comparison. Not to worry! Your technique will get better the more bread you bake, and your bread will turn out great anyway.

BENCH KNIFE

A bench knife, or pastry scraper, is a wide, straight-edged blade that allows you scrape dough from your work surface and cut dough into smaller pieces.

BOWL SCRAPER

Shaped similarly to a bench knife, but made of flexible plastic or silicon, a bowl scraper allows you to easily transfer dough out of your mixing bowl without damaging its structure. You can use a silicon spatula instead, but be careful not to deflate your dough when moving it out of its mixing bowl.

PROOFING BASKET

A proofing basket is an oblong or bowl-shaped basket lined with linen used for the final proofing stage of your dough. You can substitute using a small mixing bowl or loaf pan lined with a cloth napkin.

11:30 a.m.—Divide & Pre-Shape

Using a bowl scraper or silicon spatula, separate the dough from the bowl, and flip it over onto a floured work surface. The dough should release, but you might need to coax it from the bottom of the bowl with your scraper. Move quickly, and allow gravity to do most of the work. Using a bench knife and a floured kitchen scale, divide the dough into two equally sized dough balls. You will work with one dough ball at a time.

Your dough should now be resting on your floured board. Dust your hands and bench knife with flour. Push your bench knife underneath the dough and flip it over. The floured surface of the dough should now be on top, while the sticky top side is now on the bottom.

The floured surface forms a "skin" that will become the exterior crust of your bread, while the sticky dough on the bottom will get tucked inside to form the chewy interior of the loaf. Your goal here is to shape the dough into a generally round shape, with enough tension across the surface for it to hold its form.

To shape the dough, take the bench knife in your dominant hand. Allow your empty hand to rest lightly on the surface of the dough. Be gentle and swift when performing the following motion:

Place the blade edge of the bench knife against the board and hold it at a shallow angle. Push the bench knife away from you and up against the dough. Use your empty hand to provide traction and keep the dough in place. Without losing contact with the board, turn the blade of the bench knife back toward you, making a rainbow shape with the motion.

Use your empty hand to rotate the dough, gently tucking the dough in around the edges with your fingertips as you do. You'll notice that the sticky bottom side anchors the dough to your work surface, providing further traction. This helps the dough ball to plump and the floured surface skin to stretch tight.

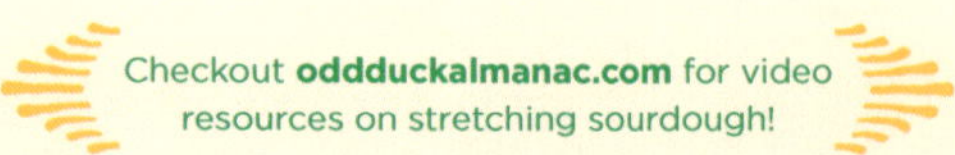

Repeat this motion several times, gently rotating the dough with each pass. Continue shaping until any sticky dough is entirely tucked up and in, and the floured surface on top is taut and smooth. Be careful not to overwork the dough or tear the surface skin.

Repeat this process with the second dough ball, then rest them both on your board covered in a dishtowel for 30 minutes.

12:00 p.m.—Final Shaping

Lightly flour your work surface and your hands. Slide your bench knife under the rested, pre-shaped dough ball. Flip it over so the seam is facing up.

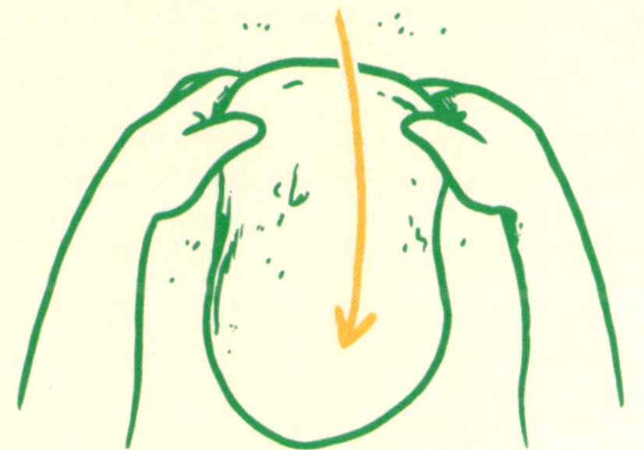

Pick up the top edge of the dough and fold it toward you.

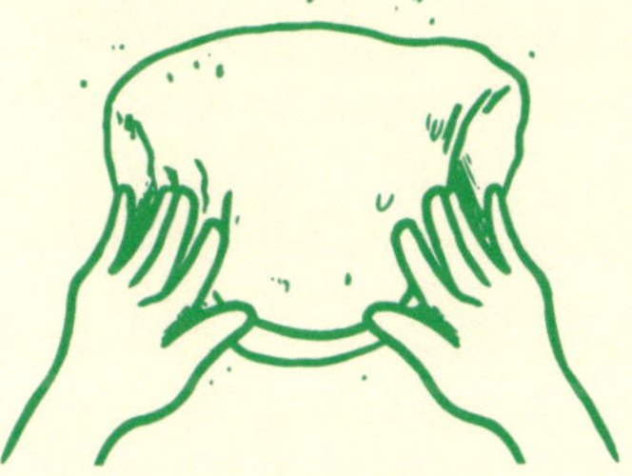

Fold it about halfway over, and press the dough together firmly with your fingers. Be careful not to poke through the dough.

The top edge of the dough now has two corners. Take one of the corners and stretch it at a 45-degree angle to the opposite side of the dough.

Repeat with the other corner, crossing the stretched dough over to form an X.

Now you've formed two new corners on opposite sides of the dough. Stretch them in the same crisscross fashion.

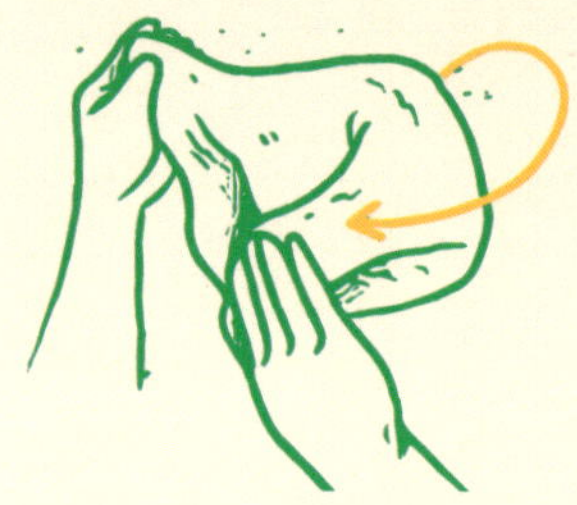

Repeat this crisscross stretching all the way down.

Take the bottom edge and roll it away from you over the crisscrossed seam, tucking with your fingertips as you go.

Roll it tight like a burrito. Your dough ball should now have a strong horizontal seam

When you reach the top, keep rolling until the seam is underneath the dough ball. Let it rest while you repeat the shaping process with your second dough ball.

To transfer your shaped dough into the proofing baskets, make sure the blade of your bench knife is parallel to the seam the dough is resting on. With your hand on the opposite side of the dough to keep it in place, push your bench knife under the dough and flip it seam side up into your hand. Gently transfer the dough into the proofing basket, seam-side up, and put it in the fridge.

The dough needs to proof in the fridge for at least 8 hours, but can go as long as 24 hours. For this schedule, we're going to wait until the next day to bake. The longer it can proof, the better!

Skip to page 150 for the next step in the process, or see the whole recipe on page 163.

STRESS BAKING

We know it's not just us — and maybe some clever person already pointed this out to you — but have you ever noticed that "stressed" spelled backwards is "desserts?" Coincidence? Probably. But we're rolling with it, and it turns out there's some good evidence to suggest that baking is a great way to reduce anxiety.

Baking as therapy is nothing new, but since the onset of 2020, it seems like everyone is dusting off their stand mixers and warming up their ovens. With good reason: beyond distracting us from the infinite doom scroll on our phones, the task of baking, of following an exacting recipe, allows us to cultivate mindfulness, to live more in the present moment. It provides a sense of routine to help us organize our minds during times that might otherwise feel like a chaotic mess.

Our brains are wired such that our sense of smell is most associated with memory, and aromas like baking bread, cinnamon, and vanilla often recall more comforting moments. We also enjoy a big serotonin buzz when we make something from scratch and create something tangible, like a beautiful cake or a batch of gooey cookies, to show for it. Posting your sweet trophies on social media not only brings an endorphin hit when you're rewarded with likes and adoring comments, but also helps foster a sense of connection with the world outside that has nothing to do with all the stressors we feel elsewhere.

And let's not forget the obvious: delicious baked goods are themselves a comfort to eat, and it feels great to share them with friends, family, and neighbors. Baking, my friends, equals joy. Jump right in and start baking away the pandemic jitters. Now more than ever, no one will judge you for making yourself a personal sheet cake or a side of pastry cream. It's all in the name of good mental health.

Stress Baking Mix-and-Match

We've designed this part of the *Almanac* as a choose-your-own-adventure of sweet treats. When we create a dessert dish at the restaurants, we're looking not only for delicious flavors, but a balance of temperatures and textures as well. To create a fully realized dessert dish, you'll start by choosing a base dessert. Then, you'll pick a few saucy elements and build your flavor palette. Finally, you'll pick a crunchy component or two for a textural contrast.

BASE DESERT

PICK 1

- ☐ Chocolate Chip Cookies (pg 54)
- ☐ Brownie (pg 125)
- ☐ Brown Butter Cake (pg 123)
- ☐ Panna Cotta (pg 126)
- ☐ Buttermilk Pies (pg 109)
- ☐ Crème Caramel*
- ☐ Pot de Creme*
- ☐ Chocolate Mousse*

SAUCY THINGS

PICK 1 TO 3

- ☐ Citrus Curd (pg 127)
- ☐ Chocolate Ganache (pg 129)
- ☐ Pecan Bourbon Glaze (pg 132)
- ☐ Seasonal Fruit Jam (pg 56)
- ☐ Caramel Sauce (pg 130)
- ☐ Crème Anglaise*
- ☐ Buttercream Frosting*
- ☐ Pastry Cream*
- ☐ Chocolate Mousse*
- ☐ Ice Cream*

CRUNCHY THINGS

PICK 1 TO 2

- ☐ Candied nuts or seeds (pg 142)
- ☐ Granola (pg 59)
- ☐ Streusel (pg 131)
- ☐ Puffed rice and grains (pg 27)
- ☐ Popcorn (pg 57)
- ☐ Caramel corn (pg 58)
- ☐ Cracker Jacks (pg 58)
- ☐ Meringue*

*Recipe available in our zine, *The Miracle of Crème Anglaise,* for sale at oddduckalmanac.com.

BROWN BUTTER TEXAS SHEET CAKE

This recipe makes a great, all-purpose vanilla cake, but the nutty brown butter really takes it to the next level. You can double the recipe to make a layer cake, and choose items like citrus curd, fruit jam, buttercream frosting, or pastry cream as filling.

If you want to make it a chocolate cake, sift about 50g (⅔ cup) of high-fat cocoa powder into the flour. Take it a step further and make it an authentic Texas Sheet Cake by glazing it with Chocolate Ganache (pg 129) and crumbling Candied Pecans (pg 142) over top.

275g (2½ sticks) butter, divided in half, room temperature
250g (1¼ cups) granulated sugar
90g (¼ cup) brown sugar, packed
4 eggs, room temperature
350g (1½ cups) buttermilk, room temperature
15g (1 tbsp) vanilla extract
280g (2¼ cups) all-purpose flour
2g (¼ tsp) cinnamon, ground
8g (1¾ tsp) baking soda
4g (¾ tsp) kosher salt

Brown half the butter over medium heat, swirling regularly for 5 to 8 minutes until foam subsides and the milk solids have turned a toasty golden color. Remove from heat and transfer immediately to a clean bowl. Cool to room temperature.

Heat your oven to 350ºF. Sift flour and cinnamon together and set aside.

Combine sugar, baking soda, and salt in the bowl of a stand mixer, adding both the browned and softened butter last. Using the paddle attachment, mix the butter into the sugar mixture on low until combined. Turn the speed up to medium and cream until light and fluffy, scraping the sides of the bowl and the paddle about halfway through, about 5 minutes total. Add vanilla, then add eggs one at a time, completely mixing in one egg before you add the next. Scrape the sides of the bowl as needed to ensure uniformity.

Reduce the speed to low and sprinkle in about a third of the flour mixture. Then pour about a third of the buttermilk down the inside of the bowl. Alternate between the two, letting each addition just incorporate before adding the next, until the batter is smooth.

Line a 9" by 13" cake pan with parchment, and lightly coat it with nonstick cooking spray. Spread batter into an even layer and bake, rotating the pan halfway through, until the cake is golden brown on top and a tester in the center comes out clean, 20 to 25 minutes total. Let cool before lifting the cake out of the pan.

BROWNIES

The best brownies are chewy, super chocolatey, and dense. Tamping the brownies down halfway through the bake helps achieve the exact right texture. Add some chopped nuts to the recipe for crunch, or glaze the top of the brownies with *Chocolate Ganache* (pg 129) once they've cooled.

275g (2½ sticks) butter, room temperature
225g dark chocolate, chopped
4g (1 tsp) kosher salt
6 eggs, room temperature
350g (1¾ cups) granulated sugar
150g (⅔ cup) dark brown sugar, packed
5g (1 tsp) vanilla
115g (1¼ cups) cocoa powder
20g (1 tbsp + 1 tsp) Espresso Powder (pg 22)
125g (1 cup) all-purpose flour
100g bittersweet chocolate, chopped

Heat your oven to 325ºF. Sift together the flour, cocoa powder, and espresso powder, and set aside.

In a medium sauce pot, bring a few inches of water to a simmer. In a metal mixing bowl, add the dark chocolate and butter and place over simmering water. Melt the chocolate and butter together, whisking regularly until fully melted and combined. Keep the mixture warm enough to pour.

Add both sugars and salt to the bowl of a stand mixer equipped with the whisk attachment. At medium speed, add the eggs one at a time, then the vanilla, and beat until it forms full ribbons, about 8 to 10 minutes.

Replace the whisk attachment with the paddle. At low speed, stream in the warm chocolate mixture. Gradually add the sifted dry ingredients until fully incorporated. Remove the bowl from the stand mixer and stir in the chopped bittersweet chocolate.

Line 9″ by 13″ baking pan with parchment and pour in the batter. Bake for 15 minutes, then remove from the oven and tamp down by tapping the bottom of the baking pan against the counter once or twice. Bake for 15 more minutes until the middle is just firm. Cool before lifting the brownies out of the baking dish and cutting into squares.

PANNA COTTA

This no-bake dessert is really easy, but always comes across as super elegant and impressive. As you're dissolving the sugar, you can add flavoring ingredients like citrus zest and/or juice (see *Meyer Lemon Panna Cotta*, pg 161); baking spices, like cinnamon; cocoa and/or Espresso Powder (pg 22); or fresh herbs, like mint and thyme. You can also brew tea in the hot cream, or steep in toasted rice like we've done at Barley Swine.

1 envelope (about 1 tbsp) powdered gelatin
250g (1 cup) whole milk
500g (2 cups) heavy cream
65g (⅓ cup) sugar
5g (1 tsp) vanilla extract; or one vanilla bean, seeds scraped from pods

This no-bake dessert is really easy, but always comes across as super elegant and impressive.

Pour milk into a small saucepan and sprinkle gelatin over the surface. Let stand for a minute or two to bloom, then heat on low, stirring occasionally for about 2 minutes. Don't let the milk get too hot. If it's steaming, it's too hot and you should remove the pan from the heat. The mixture is ready when it feels smooth when rubbed between your fingers. Set aside.

In a larger saucepan, heat the cream and vanilla (extract or seeds). Once hot, stir in the sugar until dissolved, about 2 minutes. Bring to a boil, then immediately remove from heat. Whisk in the milk and gelatin mixture.

Divide between eight ramekins and cool to room temperature. Cover with plastic wrap pressed to the surface of the panna cotta and chill at least 4 hours. We recommend making the recipe the day before you plan to serve it, chilling overnight.

When ready to serve, dip the ramekins one at a time into a bowl of hot water for a few quick seconds. Run a knife around the edge of the ramekin, then turn out the panna cotta onto a plate. Alternatively, you can set the panna cotta in bowls or glassware of your choosing, and serve as-is.

LEMON CURD

You can use any kind of citrus juice to make this curd, but you will need to adjust the sugar level depending on how sweet the fruit is. Orange curd, for instance, will need about half as much sugar, while Key lime or yuzu curd will need about the same amount called for in this recipe.

125g (½ cup) lemon juice
zest of 2 lemons
6 egg yolks
200g (1 cup) sugar
1 stick of butter, cold and cut into chunks
a pinch of salt

In a food processor, whizz together the sugar and lemon zest. Set aside.

On your counter, rest a 2-quart sauce pot on top of a moist folded kitchen towel to keep the pot in place. Add the egg yolks and begin whisking. Add the sugar and whisk vigorously until the mixture has lightened in color and is uniformly creamy. Continue whisking as you stream in the lemon juice, mixing until fully combined.

Place the sauce pot over low heat and whisk continuously until the curd thickens and begins to slowly bubble, about 7 to 10 minutes. Make sure you're periodically scraping down the sides of the pot, and check that your heat is low enough to keep the curd from scorching. The curd is ready when it clings in place to the back of a wooden spoon.

Remove from heat, add a pinch of salt, and whisk in the cold butter one chunk at a time until fully emulsified. Transfer the curd to a canning jar and chill before serving.

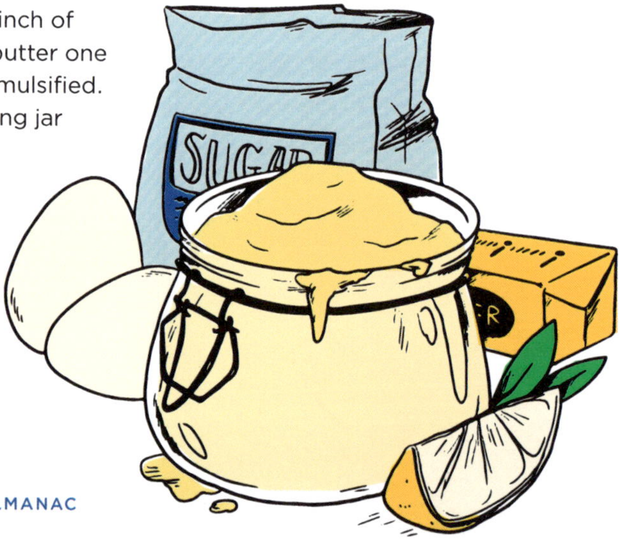

CHOCOLATE GANACHE

Ganache is among the most versatile staples in any pastry kitchen. We use it as a gooey glaze to drizzle over berries or skim over top of our brownies. It also makes a beautiful cake frosting, or we can roll it into decadent truffles. While the ingredients and techniques are the same for all of these applications, the difference lies in their proportions, which we measure by weight.

Ingredients:
Heavy cream, room temperature
Bittersweet or dark chocolate

Proportions by weight, chocolate to dairy:
1:1—for glazes and cake fillings
1:2—for frosting
2:1—for truffles

Add chocolate to a heatproof bowl. In a saucepan, bring the cream to a low boil. Once bubbling, pour the hot cream over the chocolate to melt it, stirring until the mixture comes together.

For glaze: Drizzle warm over berries or as a dessert sauce, or skim warm over brownies or cakes as a topping.

For frosting: Cool to room temperature before spreading for cake frosting or cookie filling.

For truffles: Chill and use a melon-baller to make chocolate truffles that can be rolled in cocoa powder, chopped nuts, Puffed Rice (pg 27), or other fun toppings.

CARAMEL SAUCE

190g (1 cup) brown sugar, packed
80g (⅓ cup) water
8g (2 tsp) kosher salt
15g (1 tbsp) vanilla extract
28g (2 tbsp) butter, cut into chunks
175g (¾ cup) heavy cream

Add heavy cream to a small sauce pot and warm gently over low heat. Keep warm. Fill a large mixing bowl halfway with ice water, and keep it icy cold.

Add brown sugar to a stainless steel skillet and shake to form a flat, even layer. Pour in the water around the edges, then place over medium heat. Cook, stirring constantly until the sugar dissolves. Increase heat to medium-high and cook without stirring until a candy thermometer reads 405ºF, lowering the heat as you get close to your target temperature. The caramel should be a deep mahogany color. Remove from heat.

Whisking constantly, slowly stream in the warm cream until it is fully incorporated. Stir in the salt and vanilla, then whisk in the butter a chunk at a time until the mixture is smooth.

Transfer the caramel to a small mixing bowl and submerge the bottom of the bowl in the ice water, whisking the caramel until it has cooled and stabilized. Store in the fridge for up to a month, or freeze for up to three months.

STREUSEL

Traditionally, streusel is a baked-on topping for muffins and coffee cake. At our restaurants, we often use it on its own as a crunchy dessert garnish. Sometimes we'll add ingredients to this recipe to bring in new flavor elements. Experiment by adding a cup of chopped toasted nuts, like almonds or pistachios. Candied ginger or dried fruit are also nice additions. Sometimes we'll include a cup of panko breadcrumbs to add lightness and more texture to the streusel. If you do add more elements to this recipe, be sure to increase the amount of butter you're using.

- ½ cup brown sugar, packed
- ¼ cup all-purpose flour
- ¼ tsp kosher salt
- ¼ tsp ground cinnamon
- ½ stick of butter, cold, cut into small cubes

Stir together all the dry ingredients in a mixing bowl. Using the back of a fork or a pastry cutter, cut in the butter until the mixture is the texture of coarse meal.

To make a stand-alone dessert topping: Heat your oven to 325ºF. Line a baking sheet with parchment or a silicon baking mat and spread streusel mixture evenly. Bake for 5 minutes then stir the mixture. Bake another 5 minutes, stir, then finish in the oven for another 3 minutes. Cool and store in an airtight container for up to 3 days.

For a baked-on topping: Sprinkle over the top of your cake, muffins, or brownies before putting them into the oven, then bake as instructed.

PECAN BOURBON GLAZE

400g (2 cups) pecan syrup*
80g (⅓ cup) 80 proof bourbon**
175g (1 stick + 5 tbsp) butter, cold and cut into chunks
4g (¾ tsp) kosher salt

With your burner off, add bourbon to a stainless steel, high-sided skillet and heat over medium-low heat until vapor begins to rise from the surface of the liquid, about 130ºF on an instant read thermometer. Do not boil. Using a stick lighter or a long match, ignite the bourbon and flambé until flame goes out on its own.

Turn up the heat to medium, add the pecan syrup and salt, and bring to a gentle boil, stirring to combine.

Once bubbling, begin whisking in the butter one chunk at a time until all the butter is emulsified. Cool and drizzle over cake or ice cream.

*Use the syrup reserved from the Candied Pecans (pg 142). Before adding the syrup to this recipe, strain it through a fine mesh strainer or chinois to remove any pecan pieces. If you don't have enough syrup, add equal parts sugar and water until you have the desired amount. Heat and stir until sugar is dissolved.

**Feel free to use the Pecan Infused Bourbon (pg 140) for a deeper pecan flavor. Do not use high-proof bourbon (above 80 proof or 40% ABV) as that will be too dangerous to flambé.

BACKYARD BOTANICALS

PLANT MEDICINE & FRIENDLY WITCHERY

BY MEG HOUSTON

The Earth is wholly complex. It contains dimensions, cycles, and systems far beyond our comprehension. In my journey as an herbalist, I find comfort in that mystery. It has allowed me to welcome and accept my own otherness and my personal complexities with a sense of self-understanding.

In botany, we say that perfect flowers are bisexual. Essentially, the words "perfect" and "bisexual" are synonyms to describe a flower that contains all of the reproductive parts to create life. What's more, dioecious plants like Juniper and Yew trees will sometimes switch genders over the course of their lifetimes.

Plants and people aren't very different. Each being has their own scent, their own flair or flower, their own unique habitat, and relatives in other bioregions. As children, we tend to see ourselves reflected in nature, and we often experience nature as a magical realm. Rocks can be fantastical creatures, or flowers can be used to create potions, and we are the little witches that conjure this all into being. We have untethered imaginations before we learn to dissect, name, and categorize everything.

Growing up in the South, I was the gay little beauty queen of Arkansas. Because I was femme and deeply loved flowers and frills, hiding my queerness was easy. Eventually, though, concealing my personal truth became deeply wounding. Lucky for me, I came out to a very accepting family when I was 18 years old. Embracing myself fully also meant beginning to see the illuminated common threads between my own experience and that of nature.

I come from a lineage of herbalists on both sides of my family. The medicine and magic of plants has been part of my language since childhood. My grandmother would tell me stories as a little girl about her grandmother, who would mash herbs into a paste to treat burns and scrapes, saying a prayer quietly as she worked with the plants. When the moon was full, my grandmother would invite friends over to gather outside in ceremony.

Herbalists don't study plants alone. We are steeped in anatomy and physiology, phytochemistry, biology, and pathology. We are curious creatures who love science and magic, and we work with both as tools for healing. My love for the Earth, and particularly plants, is translated through the medicine I make and grow.

I work with the leaves and flowers of passionflower as a tea or tincture for panic attacks, insomnia, nervousness & restlessness.

Fortifying and soothing our nervous systems is incredibly important for our health and happiness. Many of us, however, are surviving in a constant state of high stress, especially now. This affects how we process our food, our emotions, and the toxins that find their way into our bodies.

Nervines are herbal medicines that soothe, relax, and often induce sleep. I use nervines to keep my nervous system calm. Two of my favorite nervines are abundant here in Austin: passionflower *(Passiflora spp.)* and mimosa trees *(Albizia julibrissin)*. I work with the leaves and flowers of passionflower as a tea or tincture for panic attacks, insomnia, nervousness, and restlessness. Mimosa (bark and blossom), known as the Tree of Happiness in traditional Chinese medicine, helps us to process grief, cope with trauma, and find a light-hearted giddiness of the spirit. I love combining these two Southern medicinals for the ultimate nervous system tincture.

To make your tincture, you can play with this good ole' folk-style method. To extract the medicinal constituents from the plants, use a loose ratio of 1 part plant material to 2 parts menstruum (spirits like vodka, tequila, or brandy).

"KEEP CALM AND CARRY ON" FOLK TINCTURE

Fill a canning jar with chopped (macerated) plant material, pushing down to make room for the menstruum.

With your spirit of choice, fill the jar until the menstruum covers the plant material completely. You will likely need to add more alcohol as the plant absorbs the liquid. You can place a river stone on top to hold down the plant material if needed.

Label your tincture! The name of the plant, the date, and any additional information that feels special, like the placement of certain planets, or the place where the herbs were harvested.

Keep in a cool, dark place for 4 to 6 weeks. Shake the jar once a day. I like to follow a full moon cycle with my medicine, beginning the extraction process during a full moon, and waiting until the next full moon to strain the infused menstruum.

Using cheesecloth and a fine mesh sieve, strain the medicine. The plant material left over is called the "marc" and can be composted.

Take 1 to 2 droppersful (30 to 60 drops) twice a day, or as needed when you're feeling anxious or stressed out.

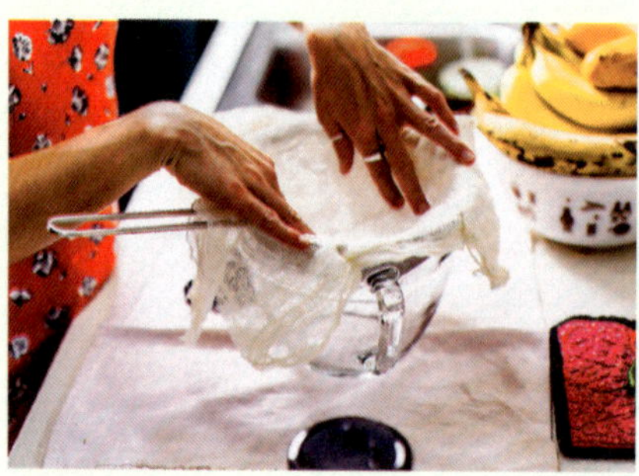

Virtually Happy Hour

Used to be, you'd clock out from your 9-to-5 at the office, battle traffic all the way to our doors, then unwind at one of our bars with a solid cocktail and tantalizing nibbles. These days, we're still here to take good care of you after a long day, but, for many of you, the office and the traffic are no longer part of the equation. After you're done with your workday, you might just wander out of your spare bedroom and into your kitchen in search of some refreshment. We know—it's not the same.

Despite the logistical hiccups of the current age, and thanks to modern technology, many of us are still hitting the happy hour release valve with friends and coworkers, but instead of gathering at the bar, we're convening on Zoom. Even though these virtual congregations don't quite scratch the same itch as meeting up IRL, they do allow us to have a drink with friends we haven't seen in awhile because they live a world away.

DRANKS

Whether you're logging in to an impromptu high school reunion, catching up with your old roommates, or getting roped into a family gathering you thought you could avoid until next Thanksgiving, we want to offer you options for your virtual happy hour fortification and refreshment.

NICE, BRYCE

CREATED BY KELLI PEDERSON, @KELBEL.84

"At the end of the night, our fearless leader sometimes likes a good, boozy, bitter, and smoky shift cocktail. I had recently come across a cocktail called 'Jeez, Louise,' and it sounded like a drink Bryce would enjoy. All it was missing was a smoky element, so I decided to add some mezcal, and it was a winner! After I made it and Bryce got to sippin', he came back behind the bar and said, 'Kelli, what is this?! It's f@#&in' delicious!' I immediately was like, 'Jeez, Bryce!!'

"It's been a big hit on our nitro tap ever since. We later changed the name to 'Nice, Bryce' because it had a better ring to it. This cocktail is great at the beginning of a meal to get your palate ready for food, and it's perfect after dinner to aid digestion and cleanse the palate."

1 oz Meletti Amaro
.75 oz Naranja orange liqueur
(or any good triple sec)
.75 oz fresh lime juice
.5 oz mezcal (we use El Silencio)
.5 oz Cynar Original
1 oz soda water
Orange swath for garnish

Add all ingredients except the soda water to a shaker tin with ice. Shake vigorously until chilled. Double strain into a Collins glass over ice and top with soda water. Express the orange peel over the drink, run it around the rim of the glass, and drop it in.

MISTA DARBALINA

CREATED BY DARLENE LAYTON, @LONESCAR

"Mista Darbolina was the first cocktail I ever put on our menu. We have a lovely garden planted outside our restaurant, and I used lavender from the garden and infused it with local honey. From there, I started the R&D process. Tequila is my favorite spirit to drink, so I went with it! The name of the drink comes from an old school rap song called 'Mistadobalina' by Del tha Funky Homosapien. The song would play on one of our playlists during dinner service, and everyone working would say, 'It's your song!' I have lots of nicknames at work, and this one definitely stuck."

1.5 oz Daron Calvados
.75 oz Chamomile Honey
.75 oz coconut milk
.5 oz reposado tequila
.5 oz fresh lemon juice
Orange swath for garnish

Using a jigger, measure the coconut milk and chamomile honey over ice in a shaker tin. With the same jigger, measure in the rest of the ingredients. Shake vigorously until well-chilled and the shaker tin is frosty on the outside. Double strain into a coupe glass and garnish with an orange swath.

BAR STAPLE

Chamomile Honey

1:10 ratio of chamomile to honey

45g chamomile tea, chopped
450g honey

Combine chamomile and honey in a canning jar and seal with the lid. Infuse at room temperature for at least a month. When ready to use, strain out the tea, which can be saved and used for another infusion. This honey infusion can be made with lavender instead, or a combination of the two.

PECAN ODD FASHIONED

2 oz Pecan Infused Bourbon
.5 oz Odd Simple
2 dashes Angostura bitters
1 large ice cube
Orange swath for garnish

Add ice to a mixing glass. In this order, add bitters, then simple syrup, and finally the pecan bourbon. Using a bar spoon, stir the drink for 20 to 30 seconds until well chilled.

Place a large ice cube into a rocks glass. Strain the cocktail over the ice, then express the orange peel over the drink. Run the swath around the rim of the glass and drop it in.

BAR STAPLES

Pecan Infused Bourbon

100g (1 cup) halved pecans, toasted
1 vanilla bean, split
1 750ml bottle of your favorite bourbon

In a dry skillet, toast pecans over medium heat until fragrant. Transfer to a quart-sized canning jar and add the split vanilla bean. Pour in the bourbon, replace the lid, and swirl gently to mix. Let the mixture sit for 5 to 7 days to infuse, tasting after 5 days.

Strain out the pecans and vanilla. Reserve the pecans, dry them out, and candy them using the recipe on page 142. Use the infused whiskey to make the Pecan Bourbon Glaze found on page 132.

Odd Simple

CREATED BY MELISSA JAMES

4 oz rye whiskey
2 oz Angostura bitters
2 oz orange bitters
8 oz sugar

Combine all ingredients in a saucepan and heat gently over medium-low heat until the sugar is just dissolved. Do not let the mixture boil. Cool and store on your bar shelf. Do not refrigerate.

"My wife, Melissa, created this take on simple syrup for Odd Duck's grand opening. The Odd Fashioned was on our original cocktail menu, but even when we took it off, we continued to get so many requests for it that we would always have this syrup on hand. Turns out we'd created a monster! Now we have a whole section of our cocktail menu devoted to different spins on the OG." —JASON JAMES

BAR STAPLES

Mango Rum Infusion

Reserve the leftover mango simple syrup to use in other drinks, or get creative with a tropical dessert. Freeze the mango simple syrup in small batches or ice cube trays for easy use.

- 1 750ml bottle of Flor de Caña rum
- 2 to 3 ripe mangoes, peeled, pitted, and sliced
- 1 quart water
- 1 quart sugar

Make mango simple syrup: In a medium sauce pot, combine water, sugar, and half the mango. Bring to a boil and cook until mango is soft and sugar is dissolved, about 5 minutes. Remove from heat and cool, then whizz the mixture in a blender. Strain twice through a chinois or fine mesh sieve.

In a quart-sized canning jar, add the other half of the mango, 4 oz of the strained mango simple syrup, and the bottle of rum. Replace the lid and allow the rum to infuse at room temperature for a week.

After a week, pour everything into a blender and puree. Strain twice through a chinois, return infusion to the jar or rum bottle, and keep refrigerated.

Ancho Simple Syrup

- 2 Ancho chiles, sliced
- 3 Serrano chiles, sliced
- 1 quart sugar
- 1 quart water

Combine all ingredients in a sauce pot and bring to a boil. Cook, stirring until the sugar is dissolved, then allow the chiles to steep as the syrup cools to room temperature. Strain through a chinois and store in the fridge.

MAKES A MANGO CRAZY

CREATED BY DARLENE LAYTON, @LONESCAR

"I created this drink during the summer when peppers were in season, so I decided to make it a tad spicy. I started the process of inventing the build by making an infused mango rum. The drink is a bit similar to a classic daiquiri. I like to think I named this drink after myself, too!"

- 1.5 oz Mango Rum
- .5 oz Kinsman apricot brandy
- .5 oz Ancho Simple Syrup
- .5 oz fresh lime juice
- Serrano chile slice for garnish

Add all ingredients to a shaker tin over ice. Shake vigorously until well-chilled. Double strain into a coupe glass and garnish with a slice of fresh Serrano chile.

MUNCHIES

CANDIED PECANS

We use pecans for this recipe, but you can substitute peanuts, cashews, pepitas—really any nuts or seeds you like, or a combination. Candied peanuts tossed in the *Nanami Togarashi* (pg 23) sounds to us like an experiment worth trying. If you made the *Pecan Infused Bourbon* (pg 140) in this chapter, you can dry out the used pecans and candy them. Finally, be sure to reserve the candying syrup to add more flavor to the *Pecan Bourbon Glaze* (pg 132).

- 3 cups halved pecans
- 1 cup sugar
- ½ cup water
- 1 tbsp kosher salt, divided in half
- 1 tbsp Pecan Spice (pg 23)

Heat your oven to 325ºF. In a stainless steel skillet, combine the water, sugar, and half the salt, and bring to a simmer over medium-low heat, stirring until the sugar and salt are dissolved. Add the pecans and reduce the syrup mixture, stirring regularly, until the nuts are nicely coated and most of the excess syrup has cooked off.

Line a baking sheet with parchment or a silicon baking mat. Spread the coated nuts evenly in a single layer and bake for 30 to 35 minutes, stirring every 5 to 10 minutes, until crystalized and golden brown. Transfer the pecans to a mixing bowl and toss with pecan spice and the other half of the salt. Cool and store in an airtight container.

SPRING ONION DIP

Check out *The Odd Duck Almanac* website for our sourdough starter discard recipe for crispy, salty crackers to dip in the dip. This dip is also perfect for dunking fresh veggies, pretzels, or your pinky finger (so long as you're not sharing).

- 2 bunches green onions
- ¼ cup cream cheese
- ¼ cup buttermilk
- 3 garlic cloves, grated on a microplane
- 3 tbsp chives, minced
- 2 tsp Onion Powder (pg 26)
- ½ cup House Mayo (pg 26)
- A few dashes of red wine vinegar, to taste
- Salt and pepper, to taste

On a hot grill, char one bunch of green onions until they're good and dark, about 3 to 4 minutes. Once cooled, take both the charred and raw bunches of green onions and slice them into thin rounds.

In a mixing bowl, add chives and green onions. Add the garlic, cream cheese, buttermilk, mayo, and onion powder, and stir to combine. Taste and season with salt, pepper, and red wine vinegar.

MUSHROOM NACHOS

Depending on what you have lying around—which for us always includes a bag of tortilla chips—this is a great one-skillet leftovers dish to take inspiration from. Smokey marinated mushrooms and the holy trinity of chiles add depth and spice to this take on nachos, while the bright sweetness of the ginger and balsamic provide balance.

Don't feel as though you need to use all the chile ginger tahini this recipe makes. A healthy drizzle over the whole dish should do. Use leftover tahini on eggs, mixed in with hummus, in salad dressings—anywhere you want some spice and deep flavor.

Chile Ginger Tahini:
1 Morita chile
1 Guajillo chile
2 Arbol chiles
½ cup tahini
4 garlic cloves
1-inch piece of fresh ginger, peeled
¼ cup rice wine vinegar

Mushrooms:
1 cup mushrooms of your choice, whole
3 green onions, sliced
6 garlic cloves, grated on a microplane
1-inch piece of ginger, grated on a microplane
1 cup sunflower oil
1 cup balsamic vinegar
Zest of ½ an orange

Final build:
Tortilla chips
Nanami Togarashi (pg 23), to taste
½ cup Oaxaca cheese
A variety of fresh, seasonal herbs, roughly chopped

Make the marinade for the mushrooms: Sauté the grated garlic, grated ginger, and green onion in a large skillet over medium heat, about 4 minutes. Add in sunflower oil and toast until golden brown. Keep everything moving to make sure nothing sticks. Remove from the heat and cool, then add the balsamic vinegar and orange zest. Marinate the mushrooms in the mixture for 1 hour.

Make the Chile Ginger Tahini: Destem and deseed chiles. Toast the chiles in a dry skillet until fragrant. Bring a pot of water to boil, remove from heat and add the chiles. Soak for 15 minutes then strain, reserving the liquid for blending.

In a blender, add the chiles, tahini, four whole garlic cloves, peeled ginger, and the rice wine vinegar. With the blender running, stream in soaking liquid until the mixture is smooth. Strain through a fine mesh sieve or chinois, and season with salt and more vinegar to taste. Set aside and keep warm.

Remove the mushrooms from the marinade and grill hard and fast on a hot grill until blackened and cooked through. Alternatively, put the mushrooms under your broiler, flipping halfway through, to achieve a similar effect. Once cool enough to handle, slice the mushrooms.

In a cast iron skillet, spread out a layer of tortilla chips. Top with grilled mushrooms and cheese, then place under a broiler until the cheese is melted, 3 to 5 minutes. Remove from the broiler.

Drizzle the Chile Ginger Tahini over the nachos, then sprinkle with Nanami Togarashi. Garnish with a scattering of fresh herbs.

Taking Care TO Take Care of Yourself

YOGA FOR RESTORATION & SELF-LOVE

BY ROCHELLE TYLER

In times of great upheaval and uncertainty, it's important we have things in our lives to keep us grounded, to help us stay in touch with ourselves and our emotions, and to allow us a space for personal restoration. Often, when the troubles of the world around us seem insurmountable, we have an instinct to retreat and avoid — the day-to-day is just too much to handle sometimes! That instinct is perfectly natural, but it can lead us into some pretty dark caves if we're not careful.

Incorporating a yoga practice into your life offers the opportunity to reenergize and reinvigorate. Before you can take on the important tasks of living your life in a precarious world, you must first make sure you've cared properly for yourself, both inside and out.

Self-care is not selfish. It is the necessary first step we must actively and regularly take in order to care for our fellow humans. Creating change out there starts with first allowing change within ourselves.

***Always consult your doctor before beginning any exercise routine. One size does not fit all, and the most important thing is for you to get healthy, not hurt!**

Four years ago, I picked up my life in beautiful Portland, Oregon and moved all the way to Austin to undertake the challenge of becoming a yoga instructor. I wanted to learn all I could about the physical and spiritual science of yoga. I completed that journey in 2018, and I have been teaching privately since then. When the pandemic hit, I renewed my efforts to reach a wider audience with an ongoing series of YouTube classes on my channel, Lifemadebliss. Supporting me throughout this adventure has been my extended family at Odd Duck, where I've worked as a server for two-and-a-half years.

As a service industry worker, I know how taxing the job can be on both body and soul. Just like everyone else, we restaurant workers need to take time for ourselves to rejuvenate after long shifts hustling on our feet. I've assembled the following five restorative yoga poses to sooth your tired legs, back, hips, and neck, no matter who you are or what job you do. Take the time to nurture yourself, to find relief, and to show yourself some love. And don't forget to breathe!

ROCHELLE'S TOP FIVE YOGA POSES FOR SERVICE INDUSTRY WORKERS

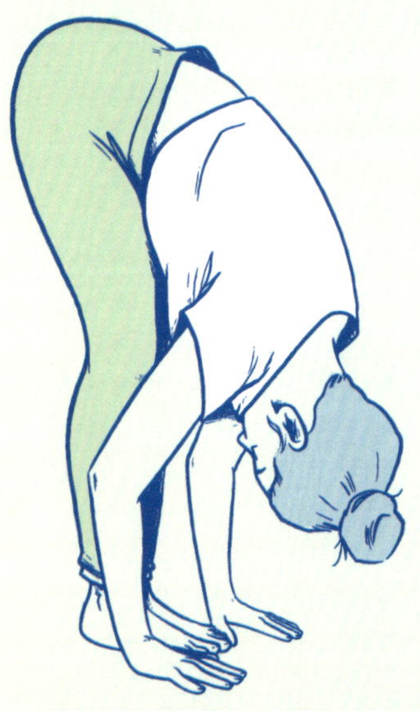

1. STANDING FORWARD FOLD

Begin standing, feet hip-width apart, and evenly distribute your weight from toe to heel. Inhale and sweep your arms up overhead. On the exhale, bend forward at the waist, bringing your chest towards your thighs. Place your hands on the mat, and relax your head and shoulders toward the floor. If hamstring flexibility is an issue, bend your knees generously. Send your weight forward a bit, allowing your tailbone to reach up towards the ceiling.

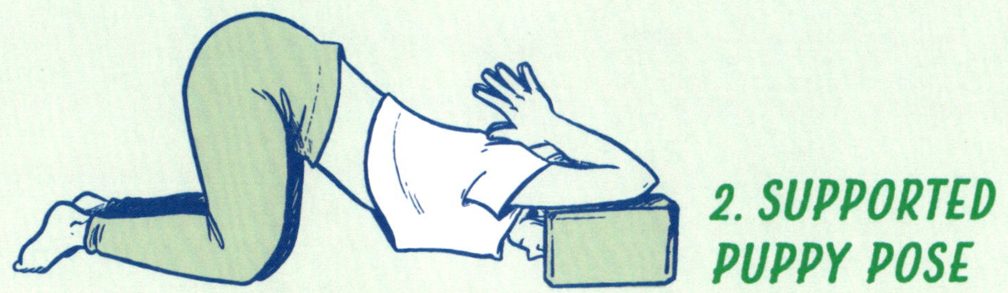

2. SUPPORTED PUPPY POSE

You will want either two yoga blocks or two chairs of equal height, placed about shoulder-width apart in front of you. Begin standing on your knees facing the two blocks or chairs. Place a blanket under your knees for added comfort. Bend at the waist and place the back of your arms on your props. Exhale, bend your elbows, bring your hands to reach towards your shoulders behind you, and allow your chest and head to relax down towards the ground. Your hips should remain up directly over your knees. Keep your abdomen engaged by drawing your belly button up and in.

3.SUPPORTED BACK BEND

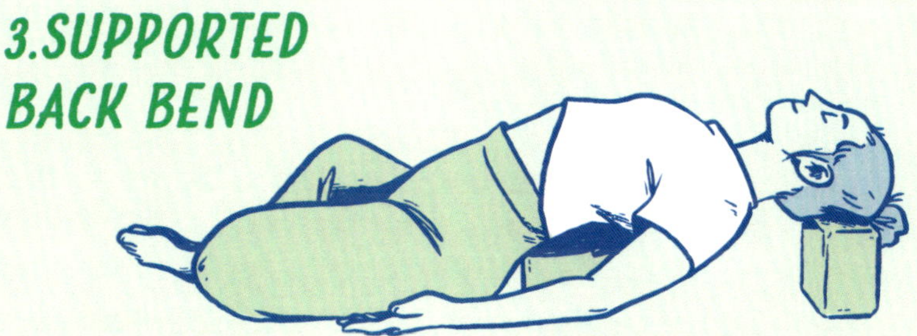

Have some yoga blocks handy for this one. Begin sitting on your mat or the ground, legs out straight. Place one block on its tallest height behind you. Begin to lean back onto the block, adjusting it so it touches right below your shoulder blades. With the other block, also on its tallest height, place it underneath the back of your head as a headrest. Either keep your legs straight out, or bring the soles of your feet to touch, and draw your heels close to your sit bones for a hip-opening stretch.

If you don't have yoga blocks, lying back with the soles of your feet touching will still be a lovely stretch on its own. You can also grab two pillows to place under each knee to help support the weight of the knees and make this stretch less intense.

4. LEGS UP THE WALL

Begin seated facing the wall. Scoot up close and walk your feet up the wall, bracing your upper body with your hands behind you on the floor until your seat is right up against the baseboard. Slowly lie back, straighten your legs out against the wall, and relax here.

If you don't want to use the wall, begin lying down on your mat. Bring your knees into your chest, then lift the soles of your feet towards the ceiling and straighten your legs. Either take hold of the big toes and rest your shoulders and head on the mat with legs straight, or keep your legs extended, and rest your arms down beside you.

5. SEATED SPINAL TWIST

Begin seated with your legs straight out in front of you. Bend your right knee and place your foot onto the ground outside your left knee. Place your right hand behind you on your mat, straighten your arm and sit up tall. Inhale and reach your left arm above your head. Lengthen your spine and exhale, then bend your elbow and bring your left arm across your body. Place your left elbow on the outside of your right knee. Remain here for a few breaths before switching sides.

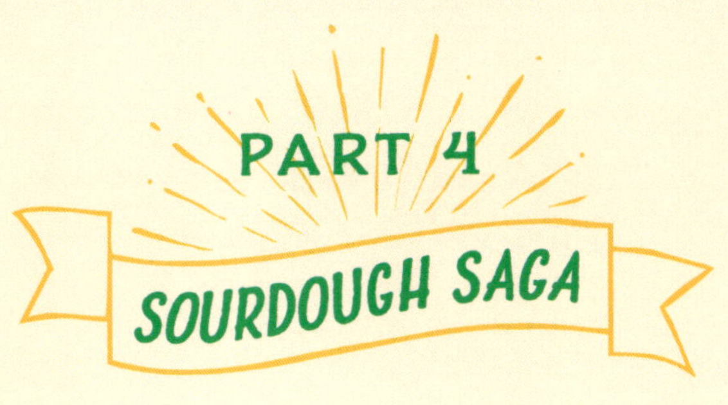

Day 3 7:00 a.m.

Time to Bake!

This schedule assumes you have stuff to do starting around 9:00 a.m., but if you're a late sleeper, don't worry. You can keep the dough proofing in the fridge until lunchtime and it should turn out just fine.

DUTCH OVEN

You may be accustomed to using this large enameled cast iron pot for braises or other slow cooking recipes. Since steam is what allows your bread to rise and expand during baking — what we call "oven spring" — the covered Dutch oven is the perfect vessel for your bread baking. If you don't have one, you can preheat your oven with a pizza stone and a large water-filled skillet instead.

BREAD LAME

A bread lame is a wooden handled cutting tool used to score or slash the surface of bread dough to help control the direction of its expansion in the oven. You can use a very sharp knife or a clean razor blade instead.

Move your oven rack to the bottom third position, and place your Dutch oven and its lid side by side on the oven rack. Preheat your oven to 450ºF for 30 minutes.

Once the oven is preheated, put a piece of parchment onto a cookie sheet or pizza peel. Remove one of the proofing baskets from the fridge. Cover the basket with the parchment lined peel and turn the dough out seam-side down onto the parchment.

Dust the surface of the dough lightly with flour. Wet the blade on your bread lame, knife, or razor blade. In one swift motion, draw the blade down the length of the loaf, just off center following the natural curve of the dough, cutting at about a quarter-inch depth.

Remove the Dutch oven and lid from the oven. Quickly transfer the dough with the parchment underneath it to the Dutch oven. Cover with the lid and bake for 20 minutes. After 20 minutes, remove the lid and bake for another 20 to 25 minutes uncovered.

When the bread is a crusty golden brown, pull it out of the oven and transfer the loaf to a cooling rack. Cool the bread completely before slicing into it.

Repeat this process with the second loaf, making sure to fully reheat the Dutch oven and lid before baking.

For a digest of the Hill Country Loaf recipe, see page 163.

As many of us have discovered, spending months of uninterrupted time in quarantine with our significant others can make for some interesting outcomes in the relationship department. We've all gotten to know our partners in ways that perhaps we never imagined possible. For instance, you might never have known they were so fond of that one pair of sweatpants they've been wearing every day since April. Or maybe you harbor a tiny ounce of regret for encouraging them to take up the saxophone again. And who knew there were so many episodes of CSI available to stream? 15 seasons *and* spinoffs? Lucky you.

While we're certain the deep dive many of us of us have taken into couple-hood has only led to stronger bonds and tighter unions, we also know how important it is to keep the flames of passion kindled, especially when you might be living with a slight surplus of day-to-day intimacy.

One of the best parts about running our restaurants is that, as the goofball romantics we are, we get to facilitate date nights every night of the week. We celebrate decades-long anniversaries, jittery first dates, and everything in between. We're lucky to have regulars who choose our dining rooms, sometimes once a week or more, to reconnect with their sweethearts.

In the current state of things, however, a lot of us are feeling a little apprehensive about enjoying a weekly night out with our dearests. But we're not going to let a little thing like a global pandemic get in the way of romance, are we? If you're a bit trepidatious about making that reservation, let us help bring the enchanting evening to you.

Start your rendezvous off right with a cocktail and nibbles from our "Virtually Happy Hour" (pg 137). Then impress with your chef skills by preparing the following menu, portioned for two. A lot of it can be done a day ahead so you can focus your attention where it belongs: on letting your *querida* feel how much you love them. No judgment from us, but you may want to consider wearing actual pants for the evening just to show you care.

These recipes are presented individually, but check out the Menu Plan (pg 169) for instructions on how to prepare the whole menu without going crazy at the undertaking.

WATERMELON & OAXACA SALAD

We enjoy a long season for melon in Central Texas, so this dish remains seasonal May through October. If watermelon is past its peak, use other melons instead. If you'd like to make this salad during the cooler season, try it as a roasted beet salad, or experiment with Texas ruby red grapefruit instead of watermelon.

4 cups watermelon, large dice
1 small handful of basil leaves, picked and torn

For the salad dressing:
3 Guajillo chiles
1 Ancho chile
1 Morita chile
⅓ cup sunflower oil
8 garlic cloves, sliced
2 medium onions, sliced
1 tbsp ground cumin
1 tbsp ground coriander
1 tsp paprika
Juice of 1 lime
2 tbsp apple cider vinegar
1½ tsp salt
⅓ cup honey
1 tbsp white sesame seeds
1 tbsp black sesame seeds
1 tbsp poppy seeds
2 tsp red chile flakes
1 tsp tarragon, minced

For the marinated Oaxaca cheese:
½ cup Oaxaca cheese, torn
1 tsp whole black pepper
1 tsp coriander seed
¼ cup Texas olive oil

Marinate the cheese: In a dry skillet, toast the whole black peppercorns and the coriander seed over medium heat until fragrant, about 5 minutes. Remove from heat and let cool, then grind in a spice grinder until fine. Tear the Oaxaca cheese into bite-sized pieces and place in a mixing bowl. Dust lightly with the ground coriander and black pepper, and coat in olive oil. Let stand at room temperature for at least an hour. Can be made ahead and refrigerated over night. Be sure to bring to room temperature before plating.

Make the salad dressing: Heat your oven to 350ºF. Toast the sesame and poppy seeds for 10 to 13 minutes. Remove from the oven and add the red chile flakes. Set aside.

Destem and deseed the dry chiles. Place the chiles in a pot and cover with water. Simmer for 15 minutes until the chiles are soft, then strain them and set aside.

In a deep skillet, heat the sunflower oil over medium heat. Toast the garlic until golden, then add the onion and cook until lightly caramelized. Add the cumin, coriander, paprika, and softened chiles, and continue cooking at a low simmer for 4 more minutes, stirring occasionally. Remove from heat and let cool. Place the onion and chile mixture into a blender and add the lime juice, apple cider vinegar, honey, and salt. Blend until very smooth. Removed the dressing to a mixing bowl and stir in the toasted seeds and minced tarragon.

To build the salad: Toss together the watermelon, marinated Oaxaca cheese, and red chile seeded dressing. Plate and garnish with picked basil.

WINE PAIRING

BY ODD DUCK SOMMELIER, KAT LONG
@ODD.WINES.ATX

For the salad course, I like a Provençal rosé, which is known for notes of strawberry and watermelon that will run congruent to the salad. Sparkling wine is a versatile pairing, a great apéritif, and it's date night, so it feels special. I especially love Paul Chollet Crémant de Bourgogne Oeil de Perdrix for a specific bottle of bubbles. It's 100% pinot noir, has a beautiful copper-pink color, and a lovely balance of fruit and leesy, bready notes.

GRILLED SPICED RACK OF LAMB WITH ZUCCHINI & CHÈVRE

Zucchini is a plentiful summer squash in these parts, but if you're looking to make this dish in the cooler months, consider using a winter squash like acorn or butternut, and trade out the mint with more savory herbs like tarragon and thyme.

For the lamb:

1 rack of lamb, Frenched
Lamb Spice (pg 22)
kosher salt
Baby arugula for garnish

For the zucchini terrine:

1 large zucchini, sliced into 4mm rounds on a mandolin
3 garlic cloves, grated on a microplane
140g (⅔ cup) heavy cream
160g (⅔ cup) chèvre
2 eggs
Grated parmesan to top
A small handful of fresh mint leaves

For the grilled veg sauce:

1 red onion
2 large zucchini
5 medium tomatoes
1 poblano pepper, destemmed
6 cups fortified stock or lamb jus

Make ahead—grilled veg sauce: Grill all the vegetables whole until evenly charred and soft. For the tomatoes, grill them slowly so they lose a lot of their moisture and caramelize deeply. When done, roughly cut the veg down to 1-inch pieces.

Bring the stock or jus to a boil and add the grilled vegetables. Simmer for 5 minutes then remove from heat and allow to infuse for 20 minutes. Using an immersion blender, blend everything together until smooth, then pass through a chinois or fine mesh strainer. Taste and season with salt if necessary.

You definitely won't use all of the sauce for this dish. Freeze what's left—it's delicious with any grilled meat or vegetables.

Make ahead—zucchini terrine: Heat your oven to 200ºF. Place zucchini rounds in a single layer on a parchment-lined baking sheet and dry them in the oven for 30 minutes to 1 hour. Chill in the fridge.

Boil a pot of water. Prepare a bowl of ice water. Blanch the mint leaves in the boiling water, about 5 seconds, then strain and shock in the ice water. Strain again and set aside.

Gently heat the cream and chèvre, stirring until the cheese is melted and combined with the cream. In a mixing bowl, beat the eggs. While you're whisking the eggs, drizzle in about a tablespoon of the warm cream mixture. With the rest of the cream mixture over low heat, slowly pour in the tempered egg mixture, whisking constantly. Add the garlic and mint and blend everything until smooth using an immersion blender.

Heat your oven to 350ºF. Spray an 8" cast iron skillet with nonstick cooking spray. Line the skillet with chilled zucchini rounds from edge to edge in scalloped layers (like dragon scales). Pour in the warm custard mixture and smother the top with grated parmesan.

WINE PAIRING

BY ODD DUCK SOMMELIER, KAT LONG

@ODD.WINES.ATX

Northern Rhône Syrah is a grilled meat's best friend. It's gamey, smoky, and peppery, with notes of cured meats, cracked pepper, and black olive. The wine's herbal qualities draw out those in the dish, while its spice accents the smoke on the lamb. A more budget-friendly option is Syrah from Washington, but for date night, it's definitely worth splurging on true Rhône Syrah. Other fun wines to pair with lamb would be a Super Tuscan, a Brunello, or an Australian Cabernet.

Bake for about an hour, rotating the skillet halfway through. Turn out of the pan and cut into pie wedges. Set aside until ready to serve. Can be made a day ahead.

On the day of your date night: Using a very sharp knife, score the fat cap on the top side of the lamb rack in a 1-inch crosshatch pattern, cutting about ⅛ of an inch deep. Season all over with salt, and let it sit in the fridge uncovered for at least 2 hours to overnight.

Heat your oven to 250ºF. Remove lamb from the fridge and season all over with Lamb Spice. Let the lamb come up to room temperature. Wrap the bones in foil to keep them from burning. Slow-roast the lamb for about 30 minutes, until the internal temperature is 120ºF on an instant read thermometer. Let rest for at least 10 minutes. This step can be done a few hours ahead.

About 30 minutes before you're ready to plate, preheat your grill to very hot. Sear the rack on all sides, about 2 minutes per side until evenly browned. Remove from heat and rest for 5 minutes. Discard the foil and slice the rack into single-bone chops (lollipops).

To plate: While you're searing and resting your lamb, put two wedges of zucchini terrine in a 250ºF oven to warm up. In a small sauce pot over low heat, warm up the grilled veg sauce, stirring occasionally to keep from scorching.

Use a serving spoon to dollop a healthy amount of the grilled veg sauce onto a plate, then drag the back of the spoon through the sauce to create a swath. Place a wedge of zucchini terrine onto the plate and lean half the lamb chops against the terrine. Drizzle the meat with a little Texas olive oil and sprinkle with a small pinch of flake finishing salt. Garnish the plate with baby arugula leaves.

MEYER LEMON PANNA COTTA

This is a great example of how to build a complete dessert dish as described in "Stress Baking." Each component adds a new layer of flavor and texture. More esoteric ingredients like liquid glucose and agar agar can be found online, or in many supermarkets or specialty stores. These components should be made a day ahead of your meal so all you have to do is assemble the dish when it's time for dessert.

Meyer lemon panna cotta:
half a Panna Cotta (pg 126) recipe
1 Meyer lemon, juice and zest

Meyer lemon curd:
1 Lemon Curd (pg 127) recipe

Chartreuse meringue
2 egg whites, room temperature
½ cup sugar
½ tsp vanilla extract
pinch of salt
pinch of cream of tartar
2 tbsp Green Chartreuse

Oolong puffed rice:
1 Puffed Rice (pg 27) recipe
1 tbsp powdered sugar
1 tbsp oolong tea

Chartreuse gel:
30g Green Chartreuse
60g water
40g liquid glucose
1g agar agar
Pinch of salt

Make the panna cotta recipe as described, but cut the ingredient quantities in half. Stir in the Meyer lemon zest and 1 tbsp of juice as you're dissolving the sugar. Set the panna cotta in shallow bowls. Will make 4 servings.

Make the Chartreuse Meringue: In a metal mixing bowl or double boiler, combine the egg whites, salt, green Chartreuse, and cream of tartar, and whisk continuously over simmering water until the egg whites are frothy and register 144ºF on an instant read thermometer. Transfer to the bowl of a stand mixer fitted with a whisk attachment, and whisk on high speed. Gradually add the sugar, and whisk until the meringue holds stiff peaks. Transfer to a pastry bag and chill until ready to use.

Make the Puffed Rice: Follow the recipe as described on page 26. Whizz the oolong tea in a spice grinder, and sift out any chunky bits. Toss the rice in the powdered sugar and oolong tea powder. Store at room temperature in an airtight container until ready to use.

Make the Chartreuse gel: Place all the ingredients except the agar agar in a small sauce pan, and bring to a boil. Add agar agar, and boil for 3 minutes. Cool until the gel sets, then transfer to a blender and blend until smooth. Store in the fridge until ready to use.

To plate: Remove the set panna cotta bowls from the fridge. Pipe several fat dollops of meringue onto each panna cotta, then use a brûlée torch to toast the tops of the meringue until slightly burnt. Spoon a few dollops each of Meyer lemon curd and Chartreuse gel around the surface of the panna cotta. Scatter puffed rice over top and serve.

Appendix A: Hill Country Loaf Digest Recipe

DAY 1 — 9:00 P.M.

1. Build 10-Hour Levain

    50g bread flour
    50g whole wheat flour, unsifted
    100g water, room temperature
    10g mature seed starter, cold

Mix the seed starter and the water, then incorporate the flour. Store on your counter overnight in a mason jar, up to 10 hours.

2. Measure out bread ingredients, cover and leave out overnight.

    765g bread flour
    160g whole wheat flour, sifted
    635g water + 50g water (measured separately)
    20g fine sea salt

DAY 2 — 7:00 TO 8:00 A.M.

Autolyse

In a mixing bowl, mix with wet hands 170g of levain with 635g of water (reserving 50g of water for later).

Fully incorporate all the flour until you have a shaggy, sticky dough ball.

Cover your bowl with a dishtowel, and let it sit on your counter for 30 minutes.

Mix

Sprinkle 20g of salt over the surface of the dough, and pour in the last 50g of water.

With wet hands, massage the salt into the dough until everything is fully incorporated.

Take the temperature of the dough. If the dough is between 75ºF and 78ºF, move on to the bulk fermentation stage.

DAY 2 — 8:00 TO 11:30AM

Bulk Fermentation

Rest dough for 45 minutes in a mixing bowl. Perform the ***Stretch & Fold*** three times over the course of bulk fermentation, every 45 minutes—at 8:45, 9:30, and 10:15.

After the third ***Stretch & Fold***, allow the dough to rest for 75 more minutes until it almost doubles in size.

DAY 2 — 11:30 A.M. TO 12:00 P.M.

Shaping

11:30 a.m.—Divide & Pre-Shape

Transfer dough from the mixing bowl onto a floured work surface.

Divide the dough into two equal halves.

Shape the dough into two round balls with the floured side of the dough stretched taut over the surface, and the sticky interior tucked up inside. Rest for 30 minutes.

12:00 p.m.—Final Shaping

For each dough ball, flip seam-side up and position the seam so it runs perpendicular to the bottom edge of your work surface, pointing vertically.

Roll the top edge of the dough toward you, tucking in using your fingertips.

The top edge of the dough ball now has two corners. Take one of the corners and stretch it at a 45-degree angle the opposite side of the dough ball. Repeat with the other corner, crossing the stretched dough over to form an X.

Repeat this crisscross stretching all the way down the length of the dough ball.

At the bottom, roll the dough away from you up over the criss-cross folds, tucking as you go with your fingertips, all the way back to the top. Roll it tight like a burrito. When you reach the top, keep rolling until the dough ball is resting on its seam.

Repeat shaping process with second dough ball.

Transfer dough balls to proofing baskets, seam-side up. Set in the fridge to proof for at least 8 hours.

DAY 3 — 7:00 A.M.

Baking

Heat oven to 450ºF with Dutch oven and lid side-by-side for 30 minutes.

Turn out one dough ball seam-side down onto a parchment-lined cookie sheet or pizza peel. Dust surface of dough with flour.

Using a bread lame or razor blade, score the loaf down the length, cutting about a quarter-inch deep.

Remove Dutch oven and lid from the oven. Transfer dough with the parchment beneath it to the hot Dutch oven. Cover and bake for 20 minutes.

Remove the lid and bake for another 20 to 25 minutes uncovered until the bread is a crusty golden brown.

Cool completely before slicing. Repeat with the second loaf, making sure to reheat the Dutch oven and lid before baking.

Appendix B: Shopping Local Directory

BARTON SPRINGS MILLS

Flour, corn products, Carolina Gold Rice

Order online: bartonspringsmill.com

BOGGY CREEK FARM

Homegrown organic produce; locally sourced meat, dairy, eggs, bread, and other groceries

Visit the farm stand Wednesdays-Saturdays:
3414 Lyons Road; Austin, TX 78702

BOULDIN FOOD FOREST

Organic produce, duck eggs

Catch them at the Texas Farmers' Market in Mueller on Sundays.
@bouldinfoodforest

FRUITFUL HILL FARM

Organic produce, eggs

Find them at the Texas Farmers' Market in Lakeline on Saturdays, or visit their farm stand Friday afternoons: 2421 SH 304, Smithville, TX

GOOD FLOW HONEY

Locally produced honey

For prices, call (512) 472-6714

Find Good Flow Honey at Wheatsville Co-Op, Farm to Table, and many other local grocery outlets.

HAUSBAR FARM

Organic and specialty produce

Order online through their Farm to Neighbor program (password: donkey): farmtoneighbor.com/auth/unlock

I O RANCH

Grass-fed Dorper Lamb

Available at Wheatsville Co-Op and the Boggy Creek Farm farm stand. grassfedlamb.net

JOHNSON'S BACKYARD GARDEN

Organic produce

Subscribe to their CSA online: jbgorganic.com

RICHARDSON FARMS

Beef, pork, poultry, dairy

Preorder online for pickup at several local farmers' markets: richardsonfarms.com

STEELBOW FARM

Organic produce

Subscribe to their seasonal Veggie Box online: steelbowfarm.com

TEXAS OLIVE RANCH

Locally grown and pressed olive oil

Order online at: texasoliveranch.com

VRDNT FARM

Organic Produce

Subscribe to their CSA online: vrdnt.farm

WINDY HILL

Goat, many other locally sourced proteins, select grocery items

Contact Ty Wolosin to get on the weekly Meat Box order form mailing list. Pick up locations in Austin, Dripping Springs, Johnson City, Boerne, and San Antonio. tywolosin@windyhillTX.com or (254) 979-1988

FARMERS' MARKETS

SFC FARMERS' MARKET

Downtown Austin — Saturdays, 9am to 1pm
Republic Square; 422 Guadalupe St

Sunset Valley — Saturdays, 9am to 1pm
Toney Burger Center; 3200 Jones St

TEXAS FARMERS' MARKET

Mueller — Sundays, 10am to 2pm
4209 Airport Blvd

Lakeline — Saturdays, 9am to 1pm
11200 Lakeline Mall Dr, Cedar Park

LOCAL GROCERS

FARM TO TABLE

Local produce and grocery delivery service, directly sourced.

Order online: farmtotabletx.com/homedelivery

DAI DUE

Local butcher shop and eatery, expanded into locally sourced grocer.

Order online for same-day pick-up at their walkup window: app.upserve.com/s/dai-due-butcher-shop-and-supper-club-austin

2406 Manor Rd; (512) 524-0688

SALT & TIME

Local butcher shop and eatery, expanded into locally sourced grocer.

Online and in-person shopping available at their East 7th Street location: saltandtime.com/shop

1912 East 7th St; (512) 524-1383

WHEATSVILLE CO-OP

Local food cooperative supermarkets since 1976. Order online through Instacart, or shop in-person at two locations.

3101 Guadalupe St; (512) 478-2667
4001 South Lamar Blvd; (512) 814-2888

SWINE
Chocolate Chip
Cookies

Appendix C: Prep & Service Plans

FAMILY MEAL: A BACKYARD BARLEY-Q (PG 97)

THE DAY BEFORE YOUR BARBECUE:

- [ ] Make the Meat Brine (pg 24).
- [ ] Brine the quail for 4 hours, starting in the morning.
- [ ] Trim the pork loin roast, and set to brine in the fridge overnight.
- [ ] Confit the potatoes for the potato salad. Once cooked, let the potatoes cool in the fat. Cover, and leave out overnight.
- [ ] Make the dirty rice for the quail. Once the quail are done in the brine, stuff them, and refrigerate overnight uncovered.
- [ ] Grill the green onions and green garlic for the zucchini salad. Cool and finely chop, then make the goat cheese dressing as described.
- [ ] Grill the shishito peppers for the potato salad. Destem, remove the seeds, and finely chop. Stir into the mayonnaise and chill overnight.
- [ ] Make the herb rub for the pork loin, and keep in the fridge overnight.
- [ ] Make the Pickled Mustard Seeds (pg 24).
- [ ] Make the focaccia until the recipe calls for the overnight bulk fermentation stage.
- [ ] Pickle the peaches and bake the buttermilk pies.
- [ ] Make the Austin Mule cocktail mixture, and store in the fridge overnight.

The Barley-Q takeout special developed in response to the COVID-19 quarantine and restaurant closures in early 2020. Featured recipes are available in the Family Meal chapter (pg 97).

THE MORNING OF YOUR BARBECUE:

- ☐ Heat your smoker to 250ºF. Rub the pork loin in the herb mixture and smoke for about 2 hours, until the internal temperature reaches 130ºF on an instant read thermometer.
- ☐ When the pork is done, smoke the stuffed quail for about 45 minutes, until the internal temperature reaches 120ºF on an instant read thermometer.
- ☐ Set both the quail and the pork aside until you're ready to sear them.
- ☐ Toast the seeds for the zucchini salad. Prep the other zucchini salad ingredients. Pick the dill for the potato salad. Cover these *mise en place* and refrigerate until ready to use.

ABOUT 90 MINUTES BEFORE YOUR BARBECUE:

- ☐ Heat oven to 425ºF for at least 30 minutes.
- ☐ Grill the zucchini and potatoes. Assemble both the potato salad, and the zucchini salad. Cover both until ready to serve.
- ☐ Bake the focaccia bread as described.
- ☐ Pull out the pies and peaches to bring up to room temperature.
- ☐ When the focaccia is halfway through baking, begin to sear the pork loin.
- ☐ When the pork is halfway done searing, begin to sear the quail.
- ☐ As your guests are arriving, whizz the Mule mixture in the blender again to re-emulsify. Assemble the cocktail pitcher.

TO SERVE:

- ☐ When the proteins are seared, let the pork rest for about 5 minutes before slicing. Drizzle both the quail and pork with a little olive oil and a squeeze of lemon or dash of white wine vinegar, and season with salt as needed.
- ☐ Don't forget to pull out the focaccia! Let it cool and cut into squares.
- ☐ Serve everything buffet style if you're comfortable with that setup. For maximum safety, plate everyone's dishes individually.
- ☐ When ready for dessert, cut the pies into wedges, and serve with pickled peaches.

DATE NIGHT ON LOCKDOWN (PG 152)

THE DAY BEFORE YOUR DATE NIGHT:

- ☐ Make the watermelon salad dressing, and store in the fridge overnight.
- ☐ Cut down the watermelon into bitesized cubes and store in the fridge.
- ☐ Marinate the Oaxaca cheese overnight.
- ☐ Make the grilled veg sauce. Store overnight in the fridge.
- ☐ Make the zucchini terrine, and keep covered in the cast iron pan overnight in the fridge.
- ☐ Make the Meyer lemon panna cotta and chill overnight. Make and store the Chartreuse gel, meringue, and Puffed Rice (pg 27).
- ☐ Before bed, score the fat cap on the rack of lamb and season with salt. Chill uncovered in the fridge overnight.

THE DAY OF YOUR DATE NIGHT:

- ☐ Pull out the lamb and let it come to room temperature. Season all over with Lamb Spice (pg 22).
- ☐ Heat oven to 250ºF. Roast the lamb to an internal temperature of 120ºF, about 30 minutes. Set aside until ready to sear.
- ☐ Pull out the zucchini terrine and bring up to room temperature. About 20 minutes before you're ready to serve, heat in a 250ºF oven until warm.
- ☐ Open the red wine to let it breathe about an hour before you're going to drink it. Decant the wine if you're feeling particularly fancy.
- ☐ About 30 minutes before you're ready to plate the lamb, heat your grill to very hot.
- ☐ Put grilled veg sauce in a sauce pot and warm over low heat.
- ☐ In a mixing bowl, toss the watermelon and Oaxaca cheese with the salad dressing and plate, garnishing with basil.
- ☐ When you're done eating the first course, sear lamb on all sides on the hot grill until nicely browned, then let rest for 5 minutes before slicing. Plate as described.
- ☐ When you're done eating the entree course, plate the panna cotta as described, and enjoy.

Mark David Buley

Shelby Criswell

Trisha Sutton

Adam Boles

Richard Casteel

Contributors

ADAM BOLES lives and works in Austin, Texas. He has written about local food and dining for *Edible Austin* and *CultureMap*. He holds an MFA in creative writing from Florida State University, and he's worked in hospitality since he was 15 years old. @adamboles512 | PHOTO COURTESY OF ADAM BOLES.

An addiction to cookies drove **MARK DAVID BULEY** into a culinary career almost twenty years ago. He still loves baked goods, especially hearth-baked, naturally leavened bread. As head of Odd Duck and Sour Duck Market's bread program, it certainly shows. His work has been recognized by *Bon Appetit*, *Eater,* and the James Beard Foundation. Born and raised in Wisconsin, Mark rounded out his diverse training and education at the Culinary Institute of America in Hyde Park, New York. He traveled and worked extensively around the U.S., holding positions in several notable restaurants, including The Little Nell in Aspen, Colorado, where he met future business partner, Bryce Gilmore. In December 2013, Mark helped open the brick-and-mortar version of Odd Duck on South Lamar as a chef and partner. When not cooking, Mark enjoys spending time with his wife and daughter Gracie Rose and playing with the family dogs, Moose, Woody, and Frida Kahlo.

After leaving a Ph.D. program in Hydrogeology, **RICHARD CASTEEL** began his photography career while working as a Server's Assistant at Odd Duck. He was one of the team's original members that opened the Odd Duck brick-and-mortar. Richard has a passion for photography as well as local food. In his personal life, he enjoys meditation, swimming at Barton Springs, and eating well. dandeliongatherings.com | @dandeliongatherings

SHELBY CRISWELL is a banjo playin', coffee drinkin', beer sippin' dingus from San Antonio, Texas. They have a graphic novel on the way, and a comic series from Mad Cave Studios called *Terminal Punks*. They've also won a freaking Ignatz Comics award with their work for *The Nib!* shelbycriswell.com | @shelbycriswell

BRYCE GILMORE is the owner and executive chef of Barley Swine, Odd Duck and Sour Duck Market in Austin, Texas. His journey from bussing tables to managing restaurants has caused him to migrate from Texas to California to Colorado and back. His work and restaurants have been recognized by *Food & Wine, GQ, Bon Appetit*, and the James Beard Foundation. He has appeared on *No Reservations* with Anthony Bourdain, and *Bizarre Foods America with Andrew Zimmern*. When not at his restaurants, Bryce can be found shopping at farmers' markets, supporting local food charities, and planning his next culinary venture. When moments of freedom arise, he enjoys spending time with his wife, Molly, and son, Field, watching football and relaxing by the lake with a beer in hand, a quintessential Austinite.

MEG HOUSTON is a queer plant witch, educator, instigator, and *creatress* who adores all things nature and nurture. Her practice is rooted in the interconnectedness of all life, and in sustainability through bioregional herbalism. She lives in South Austin with her wife, Summer, their cat, Birdie, and a tiny rotating garden. @seedofthestar

ZAC SAGAY is a passionate fitness enthusiast, and a relentless optimist who loves helping others level-up. Food and hospitality have been lifelong passions of Zac's. As a six-year-old, he would cry when given a kid's menu at a restaurant, never satisfied with the childish food and small portions. @zacquarius

TRISHA SUTTON is an urban farmer and advocate for growing your own food. She believes in the power of food to build community and connection to the Earth. @urbanamericanfarmer

ROCHELLE TYLER is a yoga teacher who helps over-worked professionals balance their active lifestyles and transform their health with yoga. She is furthering her training to become certified as a yoga therapist and an *Ayurvedic* practitioner. In her spare time, she loves to cook for others, play outdoors, practice meditation, and dance. @lifemadebliss.yoga